O9-ABI-918

Tragedies of Space Exploration

Titles in the Man-Made Disasters series include:

Airplane Crashes

Nuclear Accidents

Oil and Chemical Spills

Shipwrecks

Tragedies of Space Exploration

MAN-MADE
DISASTERS

Tragedies of Space Exploration

Mark Mayell

LUCENT
BOOKS®

THOMSON

GALE

San Diego • Detroit • New York • San Francisco • Cleveland • New Haven, Conn. • Waterville, Maine • London • Munich

LIBRARY OF CONGRESS CATALOGING-IN-PUBLICATION DATA

Mayell, Mark.
    Tragedies of space exploration / by Mark Mayell.
       p. cm. — (Man-Made disasters)
Summary: Analyzes the inherent risks and dangers of human space
exploration, from those that affect the health of astronauts to those
that result in shuttle explosions, and examines ways of reducing
safety-related incidents.
Includes bibliographical references and index.
  ISBN 1-59018-508-0 (hardback : alk. paper)
  1. Astronautics—Accidents—Juvenile literature. [1. Space vehicle
accidents. 2. Astronautics—History.] I. Title. II. Series.
   TL867.M354 2003
   363.12'4—dc22

                                                            2003015618

Printed in the United States of America

Contents

Foreword

In the late 1990s a University of Florida study came to a surprising conclusion. Researchers determined that the local residents they surveyed were more afraid of nuclear accidents, chemical spills, and other man-made disasters than they were of natural disasters such as hurricanes and floods. This finding seemed especially odd given that natural disasters are often much more devastating than man-made disasters, at least in terms of human lives. The collapse of the two World Trade Center towers on September 11, 2001, was among the worst human-caused disasters in recent memory, yet even its horrific death toll of roughly three thousand pales in comparison to, for example, the 1976 earthquake in China that killed an estimated seven hundred thousand people.

How then does one explain people's overarching fear of man-made disasters? One factor mentioned by the Florida researchers related to the widespread perception that natural hazards are "acts of God" that no one can control. Earthquakes, forest fires, and the like are thus accepted as inevitable. Man-made disasters are viewed differently, as unpredictable yet maddeningly preventable. Even worse, because these new technologies are so incredibly complex—a 747 airliner has 6 million parts, the 100-foot-long control room of a nuclear power plant has thousands of gauges and controls—the root cause of the disaster can often be shockingly trivial. One notorious 1972 airliner crash occurred when a tiny lightbulb, the indicator for whether the nose landing gear was down, burned out. While in flight, the captain, copilot, and engineer decided to replace the bulb. With the crew distracted, someone in the cockpit accidentally disengaged the autopilot and the plane flew into the ground, killing 98 of 176 onboard.

Man-made disasters are also distressing because they are so furtive in their deadliness. The hazardous radiation emitted by the nuclear accident at Tokaimura, Japan, in 1999 could neither be seen nor smelled, and the lethal gas that leaked from a Union Carbide pesticide factory in India in 1984 settled silently over the city of Bhopal, killing thousands in their homes.

Another factor may be the widespread perception that man-made disasters are worse than ever. This is probably true although faulty designs and shoddy workmanship have been causing building collapses, dam failures, and ship sinkings for thousands of years. Beginning with the twentieth century, new industrial technology, such as nuclear power and oil refining, can affect huge areas over many years when something goes wrong. The radiation from the disaster at the Chernobyl nuclear power plant in 1986 spread worldwide and has closed local areas to human habitation to this day. Finally, man-made disasters have begun to compound each other: In January 1997, a massive oil spill caused by the shipwreck of a Russian tanker in the Sea of Japan threatened to clog crucial cooling systems in nearby nuclear power plants.

Fortunately, humanity can learn vital lessons from man-made disasters. Practical insights mean that ocean liners no longer ply the seas, as the *Titanic* did, with too few lifeboats and no ability to see in the dark. Nuclear power plants are not being built with the type of tin-can containment building that Chernobyl had. The latest generation of oil tankers has double hulls, which should vastly reduce oil spills. On the more philosophical level man-made disasters offer valuable insights into issues relating to progress and technology, risk and safety, and government and corporate responsibility.

The Man-Made Disasters series presents a clear and up-to-date overview of such dramatic events as airplane crashes, nuclear accidents, oil and chemical spills, tragedies of space exploration, shipwrecks, and building collapses. Each book in the series serves as both a wide-ranging introduction and a guide to further study. Fully documented primary and secondary source quotes enliven the narrative. Sidebars highlight important events, personalities, and technologies. Annotated bibliographies provide readers with ideas for further research. Finally, the many facts and unforgettable stories relate the hubris—pride bordering on arrogance—as well as the resiliency of daring pioneers, bold innovators, brave rescuers, and lucky survivors.

Nightmares
of Space

The scene was both dazzling and appalling as a stunned nation watched video replays of the space shuttle *Columbia* disintegrating in the clear skies of Texas on February 1, 2003. Like a fiery shooting star the spacecraft separated into streaks of light. Yet the image was all too real, the bright spots in the sky representing massive chunks of machinery no longer capable of keeping intact and alive its cargo of seven astronauts. For the second time the U.S. space shuttle program had experienced a major catastrophe, this time upon reentry from space rather than liftoff, the culprit in the 1986 *Challenger* accident.

The fact that seventeen years had passed from the previous disaster may have added to the shock. Although the space shuttle program, inaugurated in April 1981 with the first launch of the *Columbia*, had never reached the promised mission-a-week schedule, it had become routine to the public. Probably only a minority of Americans even knew the *Columbia* was scheduled to return from its sixteen-day mission that fateful Saturday morning. Yet space shuttle missions, like the many other human spaceflights initiated by the United States and Russia, are fraught with danger. The hazards are inherent in all phases of spaceflight—leaving the bounds of the Earth, staying in space, and getting back home. Anything from a minor malfunction to bad weather can cause a mission to quickly spiral out of control, with the dreaded loss of crew and vehicle being the result.

Strapped to a Bomb

The controlled violence of a rocket launch is necessary in order to overcome the Earth's gravity, pass through the atmos-

▲ Members of the Columbia Reconstruction Project Team inspect a large piece of shuttle debris in March 2003.

phere, and achieve orbit. Entering space requires massive levels of thrust and super-high speeds—and thus huge amounts of volatile fuel. When a rocket fails during launch, the effects are often devastating. The *Challenger* blew up seventy-three seconds into its launch, due to a poorly designed fuel tank seal that was made even less reliable by the cold weather at launch, killing its entire crew of seven astronauts.

▲ In January 1987, workers ready a section of the destroyed *Challenger* for burial in an abandoned missile silo at Cape Canaveral.

As recently as October 2002, an unmanned Russian Soyuz ("union") rocket exploded at the Plesetsk Cosmodrome, one of Russia's two main launch sites, less than thirty seconds after liftoff. Falling debris from the midair explosion led to the death of a soldier on the ground and injuries to eight other people. The accident was particularly worrisome because

Russia uses a very similar version of the Soyuz rocket for its human spaceflights. Historically, the Soyuz rocket series has been among the most reliable in the world, and this was its first failure in eleven years. Even so, it has experienced about forty explosions out of some fifteen hundred launches since its development in the late 1950s.

Rocket failures remain so common one is tempted to say they are unavoidable—it is the nature of rocket engines to occasionally self-destruct because, as writer Gregg Easterbrook has observed, they are "essentially explosions with a hole at one end."[1] Astronauts are, in effect, strapped to a bomb when a rocket is launched, and the result can be deadly.

Multiple Health Hazards

Space explorers who survive launch face a new set of hazards upon exiting the Earth's atmosphere. The weightlessness due to the distance from the Earth's gravitational pull weakens the body. A number of astronauts and cosmonauts (Russian astronauts) who have spent months onboard orbiting space stations have had to be carried out of capsules upon landing back on Earth. Some have needed extensive physical therapy and exercise recovery programs. Doctors now say that the human body loses about 1 to 2 percent of its bone mass for every month in space. There are similarly harmful effects on the body's heart, skeletal muscles, nerves, and immune organs.

Because spacecraft are not protected by the filtering action of the atmosphere and the shielding properties of the Earth's magnetic field, they are constantly bombarded by X rays and other forms of hazardous cosmic radiation. And, of course, with the near vacuum of space a thin spacecraft wall away, the smallest leak can quickly drain a craft of its life-supportive air. A meteor fragment or piece of space debris the size of a marble is large enough to cause a disastrous impact with a spacecraft.

The risk of injuries in space is another major concern, as *National Geographic* writer Michael E. Long notes:

A three-year trip to Mars multiplies the hazards of space travel, confronting NASA [National Aeronautics and Space Administration] with a troubling scenario.

Imagine a radiation-sick, sleep-deprived astronaut stepping on Mars. Muscle-and-bone-weakened, immune-system-challenged, he faints and breaks a leg. What now, Houston?[2]

Such a scenario is especially chilling given that, as then NASA administrator Daniel Goldin told Long, "We don't even know if a broken bone will heal in space."[3]

Bucking the Odds

Astronauts lucky enough to survive launch and space travel then face the well-known dangers of landing back on Earth. Air may seem immaterial to a person on Earth but it is a significant barrier compared to the relative void of space. A space vehicle leaving orbit hits the upper layers of the atmosphere at about 17,500 miles per hour. The encounter with air causes a shock wave to form in front of the vehicle. Friction creates furnace-like heat, with the skin of a spacecraft capable of reaching temperatures approaching 3,000° F. This is hot enough to melt most metals, including aluminum.

When a sweating John Glenn, the first American to orbit the Earth, was reentering the atmosphere after five hours in orbit on February 20, 1962, he wondered if his *Mercury 6* spacecraft would be vaporized by the searing heat. The exterior of his shaking capsule took on a bright orange glow from friction with the air. Glenn heard twisting and breaking sounds and saw pieces of molten metal, from a rocket pack that had been left on the capsule because of concerns that the heat shield had come loose, flame past his porthole.

The heat shield held and worked as designed—it shed heat from the capsule by partially melting away—and Glenn survived his reentry. Subsequent spaceflights have encountered similar dangers, however, even with new technologies. Space shuttle orbiters (the jetlike craft that carry payload and crew), for example, have ceramic tiles that absorb and reflect heat rather than melt. The high-tech tiles are fragile, however, and difficult to keep cemented to the orbiter's skin. The hazards faced during landing are so abundant that early on some space scientists estimated the odds of a major accident as the shuttle reentered the atmosphere to be one in one hundred. As the *Columbia* showed, during the shuttle program's 113th mission, this figure has proven to be all too accurate.

Balancing Risks and Benefits

The *Columbia* disaster underscored the inherent dangers of the space shuttle program and renewed a major debate within the United States about whether human space exploration is worth the risks. Since the Soviet Union put Yuri Gagarin in space on April 12, 1961, it and the United States have suffered a half dozen fatal accidents, claiming more than twenty lives in total, as well as numerous close calls that narrowly averted disaster. Misfirings during rocket testing are frequent and to date have killed more than 140 people. Such accidents serve as stark reminders that humanity's pursuit of space travel remains a perilous journey.

CHAPTER ONE

Into the Dead Zone

Many of the tragedies and close calls of the early space program were reminiscent of early-twentieth-century flight. The technology was in its infancy, the dangers were not well known, and the equipment was primitive by modern standards. During the United States's Mercury program in the early 1960s, NASA managed to send America's first astronauts into low orbits around the Earth by using computers connected to teletype machines and consoles equipped with rotary dial phones. First-American-in-space Alan Shepard peered out of his *Mercury 1* capsule through a mechanical periscope. "And Mercury Mission Control," notes science writer Mark Williams, "was dominated by a huge map of the earth across which a toy-like spacecraft model was moved, suspended by wires, as the capsule orbited; on boards beside the map, measurements were plotted by sliding beads—resembling those of an abacus—moving up and down more wires."[4]

Notable advances had been made by the turn of the millennium. Many of today's space vehicles are now fiendishly complex to design, build, and operate, and they have more sophisticated safety features. Space engineers have learned much from launching some five thousand spacecraft since 1957, when the Soviet Union's basketball-sized *Sputnik* ("traveling companion") became the first artificial satellite. Yet only about 250 of these spacecraft have carried human passengers, and thus have required multiple layers of life-preserving technology. Despite many scientific advances, many of the dangers, whether due to design shortcomings or to fragile parts facing tremendous forces, remain in play.

A Walk on the Wild Side

Much of the early technology and practice of space exploration that operated perilously close to the edge could be found onboard Russia's two Voskhod ("sunrise") missions. The three-person *Voskhod 1* in October 1964 and the two-person *Voskhod 2* five months later were the first spacecraft to carry more than a single person. The second mission, which packed a number of equipment failures and close calls into its short, one-day excursion into space, was perilously nerve-racking.

Warning alarms that punctuated the takeoff of *Voskhod 2* on March 18, 1965, were a portent of the risks that lay ahead, but the capsule successfully achieved orbit with cosmonauts Alexei Leonov and Pavel Belyayev onboard. The planned highlight of the mission would be a space walk by Leonov, a historic first that Soviet space authorities were eager to claim in the high-stakes "space race" with the United States. Soon after the capsule achieved orbit, Leonov donned a bulky space suit. (Russia's multi-person capsules were too cramped for cosmonauts to routinely wear space suits, a shortcoming that would soon figure in a major tragedy.) Leonov then entered a stall-like, expandable pressure chamber extending off the side of *Voskhod 2*. After depressurizing the chamber (letting the air flow out of it), he stepped out. Connected by a sixteen-foot safety line and carrying an oxygen pack on his back, Leonov became the first human to walk in space.

After spending twelve minutes photographing the Earth and talking on the radio to Belyayev, it was time for Leonov to return to the capsule. He soon found, however, that his balloon-like space suit restricted his movements and prevented him from bending his limbs. No matter what Leonov did he could not pull himself back into the pressure chamber. After struggling for almost eight minutes he realized he was in deep trouble. He was sweating profusely and he had started to overheat from

▼ Stills from a movie camera mounted on *Voskhod 2* capture Leonov's historic first space walk, which the cosmonaut barely survived.

DANGERS OF THE VOID

Space officials learned about some of the dangers of space walks from Leonov's experience but further close calls have ensued, in both the Russian and American programs. Staying alive inside a pressurized space suit is a risky affair. Among the seemingly minor possibilities that could have fatal consequences are a urine leak (an astronaut could drown from as little as a few teaspoons of liquid inside the helmet) and fogging of the faceplate (effectively blinding the wearer). Both of these problems have occurred. An astronaut suffering from space sickness could choke on his or her own vomit. A loss-of-pressure accident, as from a puncture by space debris or a jagged piece of equipment, would be instantly fatal. When *Apollo 16* astronaut Charlie Duke fell over backward and landed heavily after playfully leaping four feet off the surface of the Moon in April 1972, officials held their breath to see whether a breach of his suit would kill him.

his exertions. "He knew very well that he might die," notes space historian T.A. Heppenheimer, "and he came close to panicking as his pulse and breathing rate shot sharply upward."[5] In order to fit back into the pressure chamber, Leonov took the risky step of lowering the pressure in his space suit. Finally he was able to bend slightly. He managed to slide into the pressure chamber headfirst, after which another struggle ensued to turn around and close the hatch. Humanity's first space walk had been a very dicey affair.

Leonov and Belyayev had further misadventures ahead of them. On *Voskhod 2*'s reentry into the atmosphere, the autopilot—the system for mechanically controlling the craft's descent—failed. The cosmonauts had to perform a tricky manual descent, visually orienting the capsule and firing retro-rockets for a specified time to slow down and reenter the atmosphere. Unlike American spacecraft of the time, Russian spacecraft came down on land. Instead of landing as planned in Kazakhstan, however, the craft overshot its target by more than a thousand miles and came down in a snowy forest of the Ural Mountains. About four hours later, around noontime, a radio beacon on the craft helped helicopter rescuers find the capsule. The copter could not land, however, so the cosmonauts built a fire in the woods and shivered in their space suits. When the fire attracted wolves, Leonov and Belyayev retreated to the safety of their capsule. The next day a twenty-man ski patrol arrived. The two cosmonauts and the rescuers faced yet another night in the frigid forest before being able to reach a site where they could finally be rescued by helicopter.

Spin Control on *Gemini 8*

The early American spacecraft, like the Soviet ones, were hardly immune to design- and equipment-related malfunctions. *Gemini 8*, with astronauts Neil Armstrong and David Scott aboard, was sent into orbit in March 1966. Like a number of the other Gemini missions, it was testing some of the procedures that the next program, Apollo, would need to use to put a man on the Moon. One of these steps was the docking of two spacecraft.

The *Gemini 8* capsule was thus launched less than an hour after another rocket carrying the *Agena* "target docking adapter." *Agena* settled into an orbit at 185 miles above the Earth and *Gemini 8* pursued it. The astronauts onboard used

▼ *Apollo 16* astronaut John Young is shown here taking a lunar jump, prompting Charlie Duke to later try one—and fall.

the capsule's array of sixteen orbital thrusters, small rocket engines to control speed and direction, to come up on *Agena* from behind and below. (The capsule also had a separate set of sixteen reentry thrusters to use during its later descent.) About seven hours after launch *Gemini 8* gingerly nudged its nose into one end of *Agena* and the first successful in-space docking led to cheers and handshakes back in mission control.

The thrill was short-lived. Almost immediately the combined spacecraft began to spin and roll. Armstrong and Scott calmly manipulated the two craft's separate attitude (relative position) control systems. The astronauts managed to slow the movement for a few minutes but then it got worse. Their anxiety growing, the astronauts decided to disengage *Gemini 8* from *Agena*. With the craft now beginning to rotate wildly in all directions, this was a dangerous emergency move since the capsule could crash into the docking station immediately after separating.

▼ An attempted docking with *Agena*, seen here from *Gemini 8*, put astronauts Armstrong and Scott in a dangerous spin.

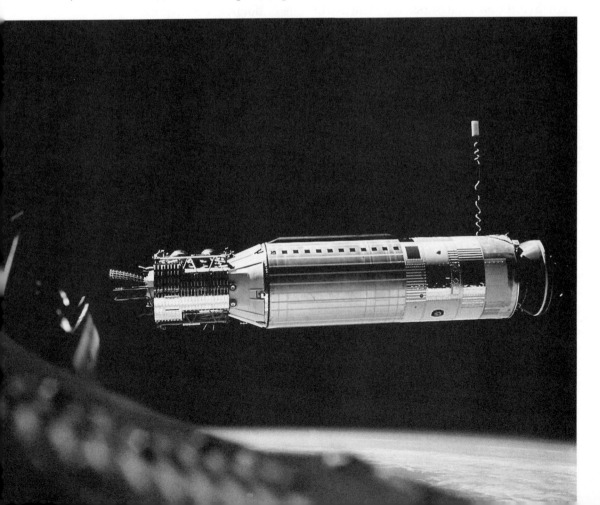

The unhitching succeeded without any collision but *Gemini 8*'s crisis was not over. The capsule continued to spin and roll, picking up speed until it was tumbling faster than once per second. Armstrong and Scott realized that the control problem was on *Gemini 8*, not *Agena*, and was probably an orbital thruster stuck in the open position. "We have serious problems here," they radioed ground control. "We're tumbling end over end up here. We're disengaged from the *Agena*."[6] If the astronauts failed to isolate the problem and control the spinning, their increasing dizziness and blurred vision would soon turn to loss of consciousness. The astronauts were the only pilots here—ground control could not stabilize the craft. If Armstrong and Scott failed to fix the problem, and fast, they would die.

Fortunately, both astronauts had received extensive training on the ground in capsule simulators. As a last-ditch measure they decided to turn off the orbital thrusters and use the reentry thrusters to try to control the craft. Thirty seconds of skillful maneuvering by the astronauts finally reduced the roll to a manageable rate. They could then isolate the problem— an orbital thruster stuck in the open position. The premature need to use the reentry thrusters immediately cut short the mission, meaning that humanity's first space docking was also the first in-flight abort of a manned spaceflight. After less than eleven hours aloft Armstrong and Scott returned safely to Earth. A much-relieved ground control hailed the astronauts for keeping their cool and rescuing themselves from a potentially fatal incident.

Countdown to Tragedy

It was not long before such close calls turned into the first space exploration tragedies. In fact, during 1967, the first missions of the next major space programs of the United States (Apollo) and the Soviet Union (Soyuz) both ended with fatalities. In part these may have been due to what *Gemini 9* astronaut Gene Cernan termed "'go fever'—the pressure to achieve overly ambitious goals, which put the astronauts into new, uncharted and potentially dangerous situations."[7] The tragedies also pinpointed serious shortcomings in aspects of spacecraft design.

On January 27, 1967, Virgil "Gus" Grissom, Roger Chaffee, and Edward White were at Cape Kennedy (now Cape Canaveral) on Florida's east coast to conduct a routine

▲ The three *Apollo 1* astronauts prepare for their mission in a flight simulator, eight days before the launchpad training accident that killed them.

launchpad test. The three astronauts, along with upwards of one thousand technicians employed by NASA and its contractors, were to simulate communications, control, and other operations. The countdown exercise was being done less than a month before the scheduled mission and required making the conditions inside the capsule as realistic as possible.

Shortly after noon the astronauts, dressed in their space suits, entered the *Apollo 1* command module, atop an unfueled Saturn rocket. The capsule was encased within a "clean room," a sanitized and controlled environment that was attached to the rocket's umbilical tower. The capsule's internal environment was then changed from regular air to the pure oxygen used during spaceflights. Six hours later, with yet more testing and debugging scheduled, they were no doubt feeling tired. At the time pad leader Donald Babbitt and two technicians were the only people in the immediate proximity of the clean room. With horrible suddenness, a fire broke out in the capsule. According to Gene Kranz, a veteran NASA flight director, "It took only seconds for an electrical glitch to ignite the oxygen-rich atmosphere of the cabin, creating a fire that was virtually a contained explosion."[8]

"Fire in the Cockpit!"

"We've got a fire in the cockpit!"[9] exclaimed a voice, probably White's, over the intercom. Babbitt shouted, "Get them out of there!"[10] A television monitor hooked up to a camera filming the capsule window showed space-suited hands fumbling at the hatch latches. A garbled message, seven seconds after the first, was the astronauts' last transmission. One interpretation is, "We've got a bad fire—Let's get out . . . We're burning up."[11] This was followed by a cry of pain. The fast-spreading fire built up pressure inside the capsule, quickly causing an explosive rupture in the capsule. Dense smoke filled the clean room. Secondary fires ignited. The three clean room technicians, themselves facing intense heat and toxic fumes, struggled to pry open the capsule. As the authors of *Chariots for Apollo*, a NASA report on the history of manned lunar spacecraft, note:

> From time to time, one or another would have to leave to gasp for air. One by one, they removed the booster cover cap and the outer and inner hatches—prying out the last one five and a half minutes after the alarm sounded. By now, several more workers had joined the rescue attempt. At first no one could see the astronauts through the smoke, only feel them. There were no signs of life. By the time firemen arrived five minutes later, the air had cleared enough to disclose the bodies. Chaffee was still strapped in his couch, but Grissom and White were so intertwined below the hatch sill that it was hard to tell which was which. Fourteen minutes after the first outcry of fire, physicians G. Fred Kelly and Alan C. Harter reached the smoldering clean room. The doctors had difficulty removing the bodies because the spacesuits had fused with molten nylon inside the spacecraft.[12]

The astronauts had been killed by asphyxiation within the fire's first thirty seconds, from inhaling carbon monoxide and

▲ The intense heat of the fatal *Apollo 1* flash fire left the inside of the capsule a charred wreck.

other toxic gases. Their second- and third-degree burns were survivable. The inside of the *Apollo 1* capsule, with its oxygen-rich atmosphere and many combustible materials, was a fire-trap. (An oxygen-rich environment is much safer in the weightlessness of space, since combustive gases would sit on a flame and prevent oxygen from feeding it.) Tests of the escape hatch found that it would take, under ideal conditions (absent smoke and panic, for example), about ninety seconds to open it from the inside. Within the first few seconds of the fire, Kranz noted, "the men inside the capsule knew what was happening—and they must have realized, at the last moment, that there was no escape. We simply could not reach them in time."[13]

In hindsight, NASA admitted that the conditions of the test were extremely hazardous. An investigative panel was quite critical of NASA and its contractors, concluding that "there appears to be no adequate explanation for [NASA's] failure to recognize the test being conducted at the time of the accident as hazardous."[14] The report identified multiple design failures and rescue-related deficiencies that were relatively easily addressed, including the need for a quick-escape mechanism, better fire-fighting facilities, and on-site emergency rescue and medical teams.

Inside the "Devil-Machine"

With the U.S. space program temporarily reeling in the aftermath of the *Apollo 1* disaster, Soviet politicians and space officials welcomed the opportunity to once again take the lead in the space race. The Soviet space program, they thought, was ready to test the first manned flight of the vehicle that they hoped sometime in the near future could take a Soviet crew to the Moon. Events would show, however, that this first launch was tragically premature.

The new program, Soyuz, was to be inaugurated with an ambitious, record-setting first mission. The plan was to launch *Soyuz 1* with a single cosmonaut aboard, followed within a day by *Soyuz 2* with three cosmonauts. The two craft would achieve orbit and rendezvous in space. Two cosmonauts would spacewalk over to *Soyuz 1* and stay as both capsules returned to Earth. Over the previous six months the Soviets had sent aloft three unmanned Soyuz missions to test aspects of this dramatic plan. Each mission ended catastrophically. One failed to achieve the right reentry orbit and

REACHING AND STAYING IN SPACE

Until rocket technology can advance dramatically, human spaceflight programs need to use multistage rockets to achieve orbit. Each stage has its own fuel and engine, which fall away after firing and then running out of fuel. A spacecraft must reach about 17,500 miles per hour to achieve orbit. An additional 7,500 miles per hour will put the vehicle at "escape velocity" and allow it to proceed to the Moon or beyond.

Orbits are typically at least 125 miles from the surface of the Earth, at which point spacecraft will take approximately ninety minutes to circle the globe. (Orbits are somewhat elliptical, however, rather than perfect circles.) Spacecraft need to be boosted periodically to higher altitudes to compensate for their gradual fall to Earth. A satellite or other craft that descends to within about eighty to one hundred miles of the Earth will soon be pulled further into the upper atmosphere. In a few days it will fall to an altitude of about fifty miles, sometimes regarded as the boundary of space, and start to burn up.

▼ Komarov, shown here prior to the successful *Voskhod 1* mission with cosmonauts Boris Yegorov (center) and Konstantin Feoktistov (right), wore similar casual attire onboard the doomed *Soyuz 1*.

was blown up to prevent it from landing in China. The second suffered a launchpad explosion. The third experienced a partial heat shield failure upon return to Earth, crashed through ice on the Aral Sea, and had to be recovered from thirty feet of water.

Despite these worrisome omens, political and institutional launch pressures led to cosmonaut Vladimir Komarov being strapped into *Soyuz 1* on April 23, 1967, and rocketed into space. Like his more famous compatriot Yuri Gagarin,

Komarov was a seasoned pro. He had been a colonel in the Soviet air force before becoming a cosmonaut in 1960. He had also already been awarded a "Hero of the Soviet Union" title, the military's highest honor, for his role as commander of the pioneering *Voskhod 1* mission in 1964. Recently turned forty, Komarov was married and the father of two.

Soyuz 1 would prove to be a stern test of Komarov's skill and experience. Problems began to crop up almost immediately. An array of solar panels needed for onboard power failed to deploy. The capsule grew increasingly cold. An antenna and the shortwave radio went dead. "Devil-machine," Komarov said at one point, "nothing I lay my hands on works."[15]

First Space-Mission Death

More ominously for Komarov, control mechanisms onboard *Soyuz 1* started to malfunction, much like *Gemini 8*. This was probably due in part to the power shortage. Two of the four sensor systems on the spacecraft also failed. These were used to orient the vehicle to an object, such as the sun, that would serve as a reference point for attitude control. The most worrisome consequence was that Komarov had to make a difficult and treacherous manual reentry attempt, using the periscope for alignment with the Earth's horizon.

Ground control canceled the plans to launch *Soyuz 2* and desperately worked to retrieve Komarov. His prospects were so bad that, shortly before the scheduled reentry, technicians at Baikonur Cosmodrome in Kazakhstan, the Soviet's main space launch center, patched through two final radio calls. One was from Komarov's distraught wife. The other was from Soviet premier Alexei Kosygin, who somberly told Komarov that his countrymen would always remember him. (Some space historians dispute accounts of these conversations, which are based not on official transcripts but on tapes of radio intercepts picked up by an American monitoring station in Turkey.)

Komarov tried to work around the equipment failures and prevent the capsule from spinning. After twice failing at manually orienting the capsule for reentry, and having to make another orbit, Komarov almost miraculously succeeded. Despite a steep descent path, the capsule's heat shield held up through the atmosphere. He may have believed the worst was over and that he might actually survive the "devil-machine."

PAYING ATTENTION TO THE IGNOROSPHERE

One part of the atmosphere, encompassing the upper stratosphere and the mesosphere, from about twenty to fifty miles in altitude, is sometimes dubbed the "ignorosphere" because scientists know so little about it. "Invisible clouds, strange electrical flashes called red sprites, and blue lightning bolts that strike upward from the tops of clouds inhabit the thin air" of the ignorosphere, note *USA Today* writers Dan Vergano and Tim Friend. This area of the atmosphere is difficult to study, they say, because much of it is too high for aircraft (the high-flying supersonic Concorde cruises up to about eleven miles) or even balloons (which can reach more than twenty miles). It is also too low for satellites—the Earth's gravity will quickly pull them to the ground. Spacecraft ascending through the ignorosphere and returning to Earth afford scientists a rare opportunity to learn about its strange attributes. Scientists have speculated that little-understood electrical discharges or other factors in the ignorosphere could damage a space vehicle.

But fate threw him a final curveball: At twenty-three thousand feet the craft's main and reserve parachutes both failed to properly deploy. *Soyuz 1* hit the ground traveling at a high speed, whereupon it exploded and burst into a fuel-fed fire that became hot enough to melt metal. Komarov, perhaps mercifully, was killed immediately upon impact. He was both the first human to enter space twice and the first human to die during a space mission. He was given a hero's burial in the Soviet Union.

The fact that so many systems could fail, and that a relatively simple system such as parachute deployment could lead to a fatal disaster, emphasized just how difficult much more complex missions, such as reaching the Moon, promised to be. As David J. Shayler, author of *Disasters and Accidents in Manned Spaceflight*, notes:

> In America, the target was to reach the Moon. Safety and common sense, to some extent, took a back seat in the achievement of this goal—a philosophy shown by the loss of *Apollo 1* to be badly in error. For the Soviets, this same philosophy had cost them Komarov and *Soyuz 1*. Equally tragic for both programmes was the fact that the lessons were not fully learned at the time, as later disasters would prove.[16]

High-Altitude Hiss Out on *Soyuz 11*

Although the fatal outcomes of *Apollo 1* and *Soyuz 1* forced the United States and the Soviet Union to "put their programs through traumatic reassessments,"[17] according to *Chariots for Apollo*, both continued to experience problems and tense moments in human spaceflights over the next few years. For example, cosmonaut Boris Volynov was alone in *Soyuz 5* as it prepared to return to Earth on January 18, 1969, after three days in orbit. The de-orbiting procedure (making the high-speed, heat-generating transition from the relative void of space into the upper atmosphere) called for the descent module, holding Volynov, to separate from the service module. A mechanical failure, however, kept the two modules connected as reentry began. This was a potentially fatal problem,

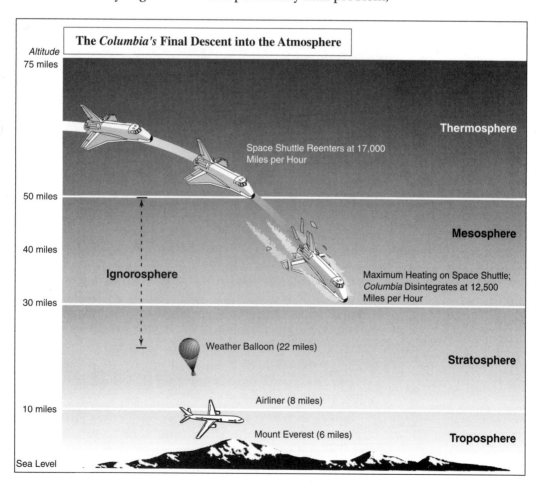

The *Columbia's* Final Descent into the Atmosphere

Altitude
75 miles

Thermosphere

Space Shuttle Reenters at 17,000 Miles per Hour

50 miles

Mesosphere

40 miles

Ignorosphere

Maximum Heating on Space Shuttle; *Columbia* Disintegrates at 12,500 Miles per Hour

30 miles

Weather Balloon (22 miles)

Stratosphere

Airliner (8 miles)

10 miles

Mount Everest (6 miles)

Troposphere

Sea Level

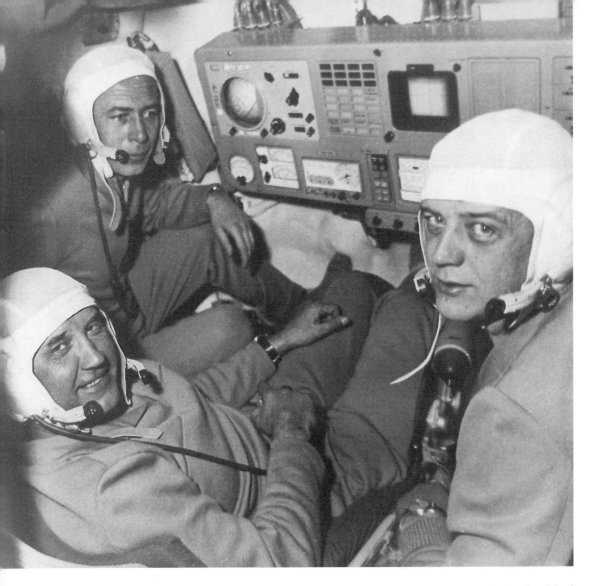

▲ From left to right, Russian cosmonauts Dobrovolsky, Patsayev, and Volkov train for the *Soyuz 11* mission in which they became the first humans to die in space.

causing *Soyuz 5* to tumble and exposing the lightly shielded nose surface to the fiery atmospheric friction. Just as it seemed Volynov would be cooked alive, the straps holding the two modules burned off and the descent module righted itself, heat shield down. After reentry, partial parachute and landing-rocket failures threatened a repeat of the Komarov fiasco. Fortunately, Volynov survived the rough landing with only a few broken teeth.

Less than two years later, three Soviet cosmonauts were faced with an even more disastrous reentry. On June 6, 1971, Soviet cosmonauts Georgi Dobrovolsky, Viktor Patsayev, and Vladislav Volkov crawled from their *Soyuz 11* launch vehicle into an eighteen-ton space station, *Salyut* ("salute") *1*, that the Soviet Union had put into orbit two months earlier. They thus established the first manned space laboratory in history, staying aboard for three weeks to conduct tests. When the cosmonauts left *Salyut 1* to journey back to Earth aboard *Soyuz 11*, they probably realized they still had a hazardous journey ahead of them. It was so hazardous, in fact, they did not survive it.

The cause of death was sudden loss of air from the descent module as the spacecraft began reentry into the Earth's atmosphere. As with *Soyuz 5*, there was a problem with the process of separating the descent module from the orbital and service modules. According to NASA historian David S.F. Portree:

> Explosive bolts for separating the orbital and service modules from the descent module then fired simultaneously, rather than sequentially as planned. The abnormally violent separation jarred loose a 1-mm pressure equalization seal in the descent module which was normally pyrotechnically released [fired] at lower altitude. The atmosphere in the descent module vented into space within 30 seconds. The crew rapidly lost consciousness and died.[18]

The *Soyuz 11* descent module landed as planned in Kazakhstan. Ground control had had no communications from the capsule for the previous forty minutes but was hoping it was just a radio reception problem. The rescue team was shocked to open up the capsule and find a dead crew. Though not the first fatalities in either the Russian or American space programs, they were the first humans to die in space.

The crew wore heavy flight suits to protect them from the cold, but the capsule was too cramped for them to be able to wear the pressurized space suits that could have kept them alive in such an emergency. The *Soyuz 11* capsule was more than one hundred miles above the surface of the Earth when it developed a leak, about thirty miles higher than where nitrogen and oxygen molecules start to be found. (The region where the atmosphere ends and the near vacuum of space begins is spread over a continuum

"A SIMPLE DEVICE"

According to a Russian official involved in the *Soyuz 11* investigation, the valve that ultimately killed the three cosmonauts had been checked hundreds of times and been used on all their previous craft. "It had always worked fine," he says in T.A. Heppenheimer's *Countdown: A History of Space Flight*. "It never occurred to anyone that such a simple device could fail." A bruise on the face of Patsayev suggested he may have tried in vain to shut the valve by hand—this was possible but could not be done instantly. Small problems with potentially catastrophic results would turn out to be an ongoing concern for safety officials.

from about fifty to one hundred miles up, while some 99 percent of the Earth's air exists below about twenty-five miles.) A Soviet investigator later estimated that the occupants of the *Soyuz 11* descent module were exposed to the vacuum of space for more than ten minutes.

New Risks on the Horizon

The tragedies of 1967 to 1971 inspired a number of major design changes in both the American and Soviet space programs. For example, the *Soyuz 11* disaster prompted Soviet officials to switch to two-person crews so that there would be enough room for each cosmonaut to wear a space suit. Over the next fifteen years, humanity seemed to have become more comfortable in space. In December 1972, the U.S. space program successfully completed the sixth Apollo mission that landed astronauts on the Moon—and safely retrieved them. The Soviets did not follow through with their lunar program but established a string of endurance records as cosmonauts spent weeks and then months onboard a series of space stations. Gradually, spaceflight seemed to become somewhat less hazardous. A new American program on the horizon, however, would prove to be the riskiest space technology in history.

A Pair of Shuttle Disasters

With the success of the Apollo lunar exploration program of the 1960s and early 1970s, NASA shifted its attention to developing a two-pronged human spaceflight program. One project was establishing a space station in long-term orbit, which the agency first accomplished with the launch of *Skylab*. It housed only three crews for a total of 171 days in 1973, but it paved the way for later stations. The other project was developing a reusable space vehicle. The Space Transportation System (STS), popularly known as the space shuttle, could act as a ferry to future space stations as well as allow astronauts to stay in orbit for weeks at a time as they conducted scientific research and launched or repaired satellites.

Compared to earlier spacecraft, the five space shuttle vehicles NASA and its contractors built from 1972 to 1991 are almost unimaginably complex. (A sixth shuttle vehicle, the *Enterprise*, was used for approach and landing tests but was never launched into space.) The production of each 3-billion-dollar space shuttle requires, for example, some 2.5 million parts. With high reliability—say, 99.99 percent—that still means 250 parts on any one mission can be expected to fail. In space, a single part failure can be disastrous. Moreover, a totally new set of concerns arose unique to huge, reusable space vehicles, including maintenance, normal wear and tear on parts, landing, and how to design a reentry system capable of surviving more than one de-orbit burn.

An Ambitious Human Spaceflight Program

The *Columbia* was the first space shuttle finished, in 1979, with three additional orbiters (*Challenger, Discovery,* and

▲ NASA embarked on the space shuttle era with the initial launch of the *Columbia* on April 12, 1981.

Atlantis) built by 1985. The space shuttle program was initially quite controversial, due to both its huge expense and practical reservations. Just one issue, for example, was that solid (referring to the state of the explosive fuel) rocket boosters like those used to launch the space shuttle had never before been used for human spaceflight, in part because they are impossible to turn off, once ignited. Ultimately NASA successfully promoted the shuttle program to lawmakers and the public as the next logical step in space exploration.

Although there were major safety concerns about the space shuttle program from the start, relating to both the liftoff and the reentry systems, the first years of the program went well. In a 1983 *Challenger* mission, Sally Ride became America's first female, and Guion Bluford the first African American, in space. With enough cargo space to hold a school bus, the shuttle was able to successfully deploy commercial and military satellites. Astronauts conducted experiments in such fields as the life sciences, astronomy, and atmospheric physics. A number of missions involved the high-tech Space-lab, an orbital laboratory and observations platform that featured pressurized modules within an orbiter's cargo bay. In early January 1986 NASA was riding high and feeling cocky, getting ready to celebrate in May the twenty-fifth anniversary of Alan Shepard becoming the first American in space. A routine shuttle flight was scheduled for the *Challenger* late in January, mainly to deploy a satellite as well as a free-flying module designed to observe Halley's comet.

"Roger, Go at Throttle Up"

Preparations for the *Challenger*'s tenth, and the shuttle program's twenty-fifth, launch breezed along in January 1986, though behind the scenes engineers expressed concerns about the effects of Florida's unseasonably cold weather on certain shuttle parts. NASA management and the federal

---

HOW THE SPACE SHUTTLE WORKS

Although the Russians have a similar once-used vehicle in storage, the space shuttle is the world's only reusable spacecraft. In addition to the orbiter, with its flight deck, working spaces, and crew compartments, the space shuttle has two main components: two narrow rocket boosters and a massive external tank.

The solid rocket boosters provide about 70 percent of the lift necessary to get the shuttle off the launchpad. The boosters separate from the orbiter and the external tank two minutes after liftoff, at an altitude of about thirty miles. A little more than a mile before the boosters would crash into the Atlantic, three of the world's largest parachutes deploy on each to slow their descent and allow recovery.

The external tank holds five hundred thousand gallons of liquid hydrogen and oxygen propellant, stored separately at a very low temperature. When mixed together in the orbiter's three rocket engines, they provide the other 30 percent of the power needed to achieve orbit. (The orbiter also has two much smaller rocket engines used to move about in orbit, and to slow down for reentry.) The external tank is jettisoned nine minutes after liftoff, at a suborbital altitude of about seventy miles. Most of it burns up as it plunges through the atmosphere, and it is thus used only once.

Upon landing, the orbiter has shed about 95 percent of the entire space shuttle system's 4.5-million-pound takeoff weight.

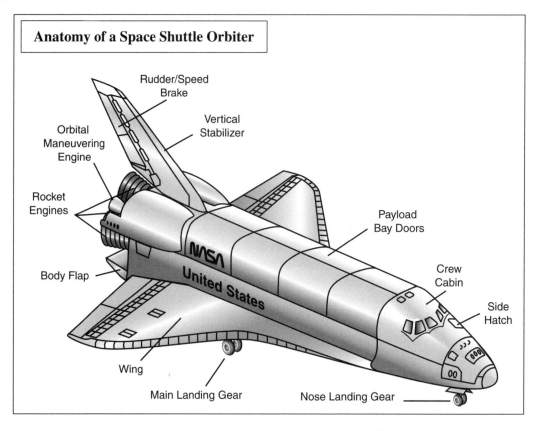

Anatomy of a Space Shuttle Orbiter

Rudder/Speed Brake

Vertical Stabilizer

Orbital Maneuvering Engine

Rocket Engines

Payload Bay Doors

Body Flap

Crew Cabin

Side Hatch

Wing

Main Landing Gear

Nose Landing Gear

government, on the other hand, had few reservations. Two years earlier President Ronald Reagan had endorsed private sector investment and involvement in space activities, saying that the shuttle program should be optimized "to achieve routine, cost-effective access to space."[19]

To demonstrate the program's ability to put ordinary citizens into space, NASA organized a nationwide competition to become the first "teacher in space." Christa McAuliffe, a thirty-seven-year-old mother of two from Concord, New Hampshire, won it. Known as "the field trip teacher" at her high school for her hands-on approach, she welcomed the opportunity to become a spokesperson for space exploration. She took a year's leave from teaching to train with the *Challenger* crew, who embraced her energy and enthusiasm. NASA suggested to Reagan administration officials that the president might want to mention McAuliffe in his State of the Union speech, scheduled for the night of the launch. Families of the crew, as well as students from McAuliffe's school, assembled on bleachers outside of Cape Canaveral's Kennedy Space Center to watch the chilly Tuesday morning launch.

People cheered the thunderous takeoff. All appeared normal, though close observers may have noticed, within a second of liftoff, a large puff of black smoke emerging from a joint in the right solid rocket booster. Seventy seconds into the flight, onboard mission commander Dick Scobee relayed to ground control: "Roger, go at throttle up."[20]

"Obviously, a Major Malfunction"

Over the next four seconds a series of catastrophic failures occurred that caused the *Challenger* to explode in a fireball. "Obviously, a major malfunction,"[21] NASA chief mission commentator Steve Nesbitt stated gravely, after a lengthy pause, for shocked television viewers. The explosion was so massive that it was immediately clear to NASA officials that all seven crew members would be killed by the accident. Friends and

◀ The faces of spectators register shock and horror in reaction to the *Challenger* explosion.

family members of the crew watching from the bleachers stared first in confusion, then in disbelief, then in horror. "We always knew there would be a day like this," John Glenn said later. "We're dealing with speeds and powers and complexities we've never dealt with before. This was a day we wish we could kick back forever."[22]

Unlike on the *Columbia*, the explosion that ripped apart the *Challenger* left the orbiter's crew cabin, an independent unit within the orbiter, more or less intact. Photos of the explosion distinctly show the crew cabin hurtling away from the fireball of the external tank explosion. NASA determined that the crew cabin reached an altitude of sixty-five thousand feet before taking more than two minutes to fall into the Atlantic. It hit at a speed of more than two hundred miles per hour and sank to the ocean floor ninety feet below, where the wreckage—and the bodies of McAuliffe, Scobee, Mike Smith, Judy Resnick, Ellison Onizuka, Greg Jarvis, and Ron McNair—were recovered six weeks later.

Close-up photos of the launch sequence helped to reconstruct the sequence of events leading up to the disaster. A minute into the launch, a plume of flame was seen in the same general area as the earlier puff of smoke on the right rocket booster. This was followed within twenty seconds by major structural failure of the external tank and then the catastrophic explosion. This basic scenario was confirmed by a close examination of the many tons—representing almost half of the total space shuttle—of *Challenger* debris recovered from Cape Canaveral's coastal waters. The orbiter and its three main rocket engines were shown to have worked as expected. The accident was due to a mechanical problem with the launch vehicles, the right solid rocket booster and the external tank.

DID THE *CHALLENGER* CREW SURVIVE BREAKUP?

Most of the news reports after the accident assumed that the *Challenger* astronauts were all killed by the massive external tank explosion. But were they? Six months after the *Challenger* disaster, NASA shocked the nation when it released a report by biomedical specialist Joseph Kerwin. NASA had commissioned Kerwin and a team of engineers, scientists, and pathologists to study the astronauts' deaths. The investigators examined the crew compartment wreckage, reviewed data and photos, and studied the remains of the astronauts. Kerwin concluded that it was impossible to determine precisely when and how everybody aboard died, since the crew compartment's violent final impact with the ocean masked the damage from the earlier explosion. The evidence did show, however, that "the forces to which the crew were exposed during the orbiter breakup were probably not sufficient to cause death or serious injury." Moreover, three of the astronauts had manually activated their emergency air packs, and thus must have remained conscious through the explosion.

Lessons Learned

The shuttle program was grounded for almost three years in the aftermath of the *Challenger* disaster, at least in part because NASA was less than forthcoming about exactly what had happened, and why. It took a presidential commission, and a persistent press, to drag the truth out: Space shuttle officials had willingly overlooked or ignored their own safety rules to launch the *Challenger*.

After consulting with engineers familiar with the shuttle's operation and construction, accident investigators were able to identify the immediate cause of the leak from the solid rocket booster. A synthetic rubber, o-ring gasket used to seal the joint between the segments of the booster contracted in the cold weather. This allowed hot gases and flames to escape from the joint and ignite the external fuel tank.

Not only was this scenario predictable, it was thoroughly discussed the very night before the *Challenger* launch. Late into the evening of January 27, a team of engineers from Utah-based Morton Thiokol, the aerospace company that had built the booster rockets, had held an urgent teleconference with mid-level NASA managers. The Morton Thiokol engineers were adamant that the cold weather predicted for Florida the next morning (the temperature at launch turned out to be 36º F) was much too low to assure that the o-rings would hold. The NASA managers brushed off these concerns, saying that there was not enough data to prove a danger existed. The Morton Thiokol engineers were not mollified, and the Morton Thiokol program manager refused to sign off on the launch, a NASA safety requirement. The scheduled launch could go forward only when NASA pressured the company and a more senior, executive-level Morton Thiokol manager agreed to make the necessary sign-off. The *Challenger* astronauts were not brought into, or even alerted to, these crucial technical discussions.

The overall effect of press coverage and the numerous government investigations of NASA's performance with regard to the *Challenger* was to be a scathing critique of the agency. It was shown to have become too ready to sacrifice safety in favor of staying on schedule. NASA was doing this at least in part for political reasons—it wanted to show congressional supporters that its goal of launching forty shuttle missions per year was a reachable one. Investigators also found NASA's management style seriously flawed and in need of overhaul.

Fighting the Odds

The *Challenger* disaster led to a number of important program reforms, both in terms of equipment and procedures. For example, scheduling henceforth was to take a backseat to crew safety, and any technical issues that might conceivably have catastrophic implications were henceforth to be vetted by both mid- and upper-level management. When NASA built a new orbiter vehicle, the *Endeavour*, to replace the lost *Challenger*, it added new crew-escape technology to be used in certain emergency circumstances.

After the almost three-year interruption in shuttle launches due to the *Challenger* investigation and reform, NASA's next fifteen years, encompassing almost ninety space shuttle missions, came off with minor glitches but no major problems or catastrophic accidents. In 1999 NASA highlighted its ongoing commitment to safety by temporarily grounding the entire shuttle fleet because of a potential wiring flaw, even though a statistical analysis showed little cause for anxiety. On the other hand, there were growing levels of concern among some space officials relating to the aging of the shuttle fleet, and to budget cuts that reduced funding for maintenance and safety personnel.

The space agency's streak of good fortune came to an abrupt halt in early 2003. In mid-January, the *Columbia* was scheduled to be launched on its twenty-seventh mission since its maiden voyage almost twenty-two years earlier. What concerns there were about its age, and the fact that it was originally built using 1970s technology, had been somewhat alleviated by a major, seventeen-month overhaul the *Columbia* underwent in 2000–2001.

A Glitch on Launch

NASA assembled a multicultural crew for STS-107 (the final *Columbia* mission's official name; 107 is an assigned, rather than chronological, mission number). Ilan Ramon would be the first Israeli to venture into space. Three of the astronauts had been on previous shuttle missions, including Kalpana Chawla, who had logged fifteen days and 6.5 million miles aboard *Columbia* on a 1997 shuttle flight. On that mission she played a major role in a number of scientific experiments, with fellow crew members often turning to "KC," as they called her, to sort out some tough technical problem.

The launch on January 16 apparently went well. The only potential glitch was that out-of-focus launch images showed a piece of rigid insulating foam peeling off of the external fuel tank and striking the orbiter's left wing before disintegrating. NASA officials were concerned enough to commission a computer modeling of a foam-impact test. The analysis was conducted with the help of Boeing, the aeronautics giant that is a major space contractor. The researchers tried to assess what would happen if a piece of spray-on foam, similar to the estimated two-pound piece that fell off the external tank, struck various parts of the orbiter's wing at speeds exceeding five hundred miles per hour, the approximate speed of impact.

When NASA and Boeing engineers analyzed the data they received from this computer modeling, they concluded that the event did not present any danger to the spacecraft. Flight director Steve Stich even e-mailed the *Columbia* astronauts, one week into the mission, that the foam strike was "absolutely no concern" and "not even worth mentioning."[23] NASA officials also decided that the incident was of such little importance it was not worth requesting that one or more of the government's orbiting spy satellites take photographs of

▲ Repairs, like these being made around *Columbia*'s windows after an early mission, are necessary on the aging orbiters after each flight.

Columbia's wing, which the satellites are readily capable of doing. Unfortunately, the computer test findings would turn out to be flawed, the safety conclusions misleading, and the management decisions fateful.

A Reentry Goes Awry

The *Columbia* crew spent sixteen days in space, conducting some eighty scientific experiments. Ten minutes before nine on the morning of Saturday, February 1, the *Columbia* approached coastal California to eventually land, an expected twenty-five minutes later, at Cape Canaveral. Weather conditions were perfect in Florida and the sixteen-thousand-mile-per-hour descent toward the Earth seemed routine to ground control and to the astronauts onboard. The *Columbia*'s computers had the craft skimming into the upper layers of the atmosphere, banking right and left but always with the ship's thermal-tiled underside taking the brunt of the searing heat.

Despite the known dangers, no shuttle had ever experienced a catastrophe during landing. Indeed, the U.S. space program had not lost a craft on reentry in more than forty years of launches. Shockingly, over the course of the next eight minutes, the *Columbia* was totally destroyed and its seven crew members killed.

The first hint of a problem came when ground controller Jeff Kling reported a sudden loss of data from four separate temperature sensors on the left side of the *Columbia*. (The orbiters have some two thousand sensors and data points planted strategically throughout the craft, to alert crew and ground control to any problems as they develop.) Flight director Leroy Cain asked Kling if the sensors covered any electronic components in common. Kling's negative response was bad news, as it suggested not an isolated problem but a potentially system-wide failure.

Within quick succession came more bad news from NASA ground officers. *Columbia*'s left wing showed evidence of increased wind resistance. The huge tires on the landing gear, which were still tucked away inside the belly of the orbiter, lost their pressure. There was a short, garbled message from the *Columbia*. A ground control communicator alerted the crew: "And *Columbia*, Houston, we see your tire pressure messages and we did not copy your last." The aborted response, the final words from the shuttle, were from commander Rick Husband: "Roger, uh, buh . . ." [24]

LANDING THE "BRICK WITH WINGS"

Everything must work exactly as planned to safely land an unpowered, one-hundred-ton craft like the space shuttle orbiter. Once the spacecraft enters the Earth's atmosphere, it becomes in effect a heavy glider—"a brick with wings," engineers have dubbed it. Computerized navigational programs and equipment onboard the orbiter handle most of the precise turns and attitude adjustments necessary to bring it through the atmosphere. Typically the orbiter's commander takes control during the last few minutes, flying the final twenty-five miles and landing the orbiter.

Picking a landing site can be a tough decision for ground control, since weather is a major factor. Once the de-orbit burn is done, an hour before touchdown, it is not possible to change the landing site. Thunderstorms, poor visibility, or heavy crosswinds at the three-mile-long Kennedy Space Center landing strip mean the shuttle must make another orbit or commit to a landing at an alternate site, such as a lake bed at California's Edwards Air Force Base. Because the orbiter is unpowered, it gets only one chance at hitting the ground at the right speed (about 220 miles per hour) and approach angle (twenty degrees, or six times as steep as the approach of a commercial jet). Most shuttle landings have gone smoothly, although *Discovery* blew a tire and damaged its brakes during an April 1985 landing. Orbiters have since been fitted with drag chutes to help slow them to a stop after landing.

▲ Smoke trails from *Discovery*'s main landing gear in November 1998 during a typical high-speed touchdown.

KALPANA CHAWLA: FIRST INDIAN WOMAN IN SPACE

Born into a traditional family in India, Kalpana Chawla chose an unusual career that led her to become the first woman of her country to go to space. By the age of fourteen she knew she wanted to be an astronaut. After receiving her bachelor's degree from a college in India in 1982 (she was the only female in her class), she moved to the United States to do her postgraduate work. She earned a master's in aerospace engineering in 1984 and a doc-torate in the same field in 1988. She became a certified flight instructor and then an astronaut in 1994. She was forty-one, and married to flying instructor Jean-Pierre Harrison, when she died.

The time Chawla spent in space reminded her of the need for all of humanity to be wiser stewards of Earth. "This planet below you is our campsite," she told *Time* magazine, "and you know of no other."

▲ Ten weeks prior to her death, Chawla floats in a small life raft during a training exercise.

A Hair-Raising Death-Spiral

The scene onboard the *Columbia* can be recreated only speculatively but quite likely the crew had become aware of the budding catastrophe and were grappling with the cascade of problems. Drag on the spacecraft's left side increased. "They are seeing multiple failures on top of one another," former astronaut and shuttle pilot Tom Hendricks told *Time* magazine. "But they are thinking they can handle things like they do in the simulator." Recovered computer data suggested that during the ship's final, death-spiraling fifteen seconds, Husband switched from autopilot to manual as he attempted to regain control. "It would have been hair-raising because he knew survival wasn't likely,"[25] says Hendricks. With one wing breaking up, the *Columbia* would have tumbled out of control, allowing the reentry friction to smash the spaceship into pieces.

At ground control, even more alarming than the stream of bad-news data was the end of any communication at all. Sensors were lost or signals cut off from the orbiter's nose and its right main landing gear. Minutes went by with no response from the *Columbia*'s crew. As the gravity of the situation sank in, mission control kept repeating, "*Columbia*, Houston, com [communications] check." The *Columbia* had disappeared from Houston's radar screens and was not responding on the radio. Finally a controller stated, "We are in the search pattern," an admission that the spacecraft had disintegrated. "Lock the doors,"[26] Cain commanded. This meant no one could leave the mission control room, or even make outside phone calls. Mission control shifted its focus from bringing the crew home to figuring out why that had not happened. Officials started saving computer data, logs, and transmissions, and reconstructing their actions, so that they could provide crucial clues for the investigation.

"The *Columbia* Is Lost"

The residents of eastern Texas were among the first to know of the disaster. Even at an altitude of forty miles, the explosive forces that destroyed the *Columbia* were powerful enough to shake houses around the small city of Nacogdoches. Many witnesses heard a massive boom and looked up to see flaming pieces of the *Columbia* blaze overhead, leaving white contrails that hung like tear streaks in the clear blue sky. Within minutes debris started to thud to the ground.

At a televised news conference later that day, a saddened President George W. Bush was forced to announce to a stunned nation, "The *Columbia* is lost; there are no survivors." Killed along with Husband, Ramon, and Chawla were William McCool, Michael Anderson, David Brown, and Laurel Clark. The loss of the *Columbia* and its crew of seven was a devastating blow to the nation and to the space shuttle program. As Mark Cantrell and Donald Vaughan, the authors of *Sixteen Minutes from Home: The Columbia Space Shuttle Tragedy*, note:

Television viewers around the globe sat in anguish as video footage of the tragedy, captured by professional cameramen and amateurs alike, played over and over again. Although 17 years had passed since the *Challenger* exploded on a cold January morning in 1986, the memories of that awful day came rushing back, a shocking wake-up call to a world grown complacent by the seemingly routine nature of space travel.[27]

The initial investigations into the cause of the *Columbia* tragedy were wide-ranging. Space experts speculated that the orbiter might have been hit by a meteor or by a piece of space debris, or that a failure in the thermal tiles had doomed the craft. A series of revealing tests soon shifted investigators' focus to the likelihood that the falling piece of foam damaged the *Columbia*'s leading left wing edge on takeoff.

Could the *Columbia* Have Been Rescued?

One of the contingencies space experts have considered is what would happen if a spacecraft suffered so much irreparable damage that it would almost certainly disintegrate, like

▼ Fragments of *Columbia* streak through the Texas sky on the morning of February 1, 2003.

▲ Search teams left makeshift memorials where remains of *Columbia* astronauts were found in Texas.

the *Columbia*, upon return from orbit. Thus, for example, a shuttle crew could theoretically be in space for three weeks or longer knowing—and the public knowing as well—that they were doomed when, at the last possible moment, their craft would have no choice but to return to Earth.

This spine-tingling scenario became more real as experts debated what could have possibly been done to rescue the seven astronauts onboard *Columbia* if, for example, NASA had determined from telescopic examination that the orbiter's wing was too damaged for a safe reentry. What options did NASA have to retrieve the crew? Unfortunately, not many. Surprisingly, after the first nine minutes of flight, a rescue would have proved risky, for various reasons. It turns out that the value of space walks, escape pods, and other technologies that could aid space rescues has been a matter of heated debate for decades, with the *Columbia* accident adding more fuel to the fire.

CHAPTER THREE

Rescue Efforts

In the immediate aftermath of the *Columbia* disaster, NASA claimed that a last-minute rescue would have been virtually impossible. Shuttle program manager Ron Dittemore said, "There was zero we could do about it."[28] Within days, however, NASA officials began to backtrack from this gloomy admission of futility. According to NASA administrator Sean O'Keefe, the agency would have made extraordinary efforts and devoted all of its resources to avoid catastrophe. "I fundamentally, absolutely reject the proposition that there was nothing that could be done on orbit,"[29] he said.

At the request of the Columbia Accident Investigation Board (CAIB), NASA analyzed various potential rescue plans. It came up with a number of highly risky and at least remotely feasible plans, most prominently a meeting with the *Atlantis* that would have involved tethered rescuers bringing extra space suits to the *Columbia* and retrieving the crew. Such a plan could not have been organized until very close to the thirty-day limit for keeping the *Columbia* in orbit. Many space observers believe, however, that it was highly unlikely that this or any other rescue plan for the *Columbia* could have succeeded, for a number of reasons.

Wishful Thinking?

First of all, a repair in space was virtually inconceivable. The *Columbia* had onboard no spare thermal tiles (since each one is uniquely shaped for a specific spot), and few other spare parts. The astronauts also had no way to evaluate external damage, much less repair it. "The orbiter does not normally carry the backpacks used for maneuvering in orbit; the belly of the shuttle has no handholds for maneuvering; and the remote manipulating system—the shuttle's long mechanical arm—was not carried on this flight because it was not needed for the science experiments,"[30] noted *Orlando Sentinel* writer Thomas H. Maugh II. Given these limitations, NASA officials seemed to be engaged in wishful thinking when, months after the accident, they floated the idea that a spacewalking *Columbia* astronaut could have repaired a hole in the wing by stuffing in a bag of water and then returning later, after the spacecraft had been oriented to allow the water to freeze, to cover the plug with Teflon tape.

It was physically impossible for the *Columbia* to have rendezvoused with the *International Space Station*, the orbiting scientific platform that began continuous human residency in November 2000. The shuttle did not have anywhere near the fuel it would have needed to rocket seventy miles higher and reach the orbit of the station. Even if the *Columbia* could have reached it, unlike the three other orbiters, the *Columbia* did not have the necessary equipment to dock with the station.

Space experts also generally agreed that orienting the *Columbia* so that it entered the atmosphere in a way that put more of the reentry heat on the intact right wing would not have made enough of a difference to have prevented eventual disintegration of the left wing and then the spacecraft.

"A Fatal Launch"

Rescue by a second shuttle orbiter was perhaps the best, though still unsure, possibility. On February 1, at the end of its expected mission time, the *Columbia* crew had about a one-month supply of oxygen, food, and water. The most limiting factor, however, was that the orbiter carried only an additional two-week supply of the canisters that absorb carbon dioxide, the gas given off during breathing that becomes toxic when it accumulates to high enough levels. Readying a second shuttle launch usually takes a month from the time it reaches the pad—certain procedures such as fueling can be accelerated only by so much. When the *Columbia* was launched, NASA had a March 1 launch scheduled for the *Atlantis*. If the *Columbia's* fatal problem had been recognized by January 21, an *Atlantis* launch could have been moved up to perhaps February 11. Assuming one day to rendezvous, this left only two days leeway before it would have been too late for any rescue mission.

Shortening the launch schedule of the *Atlantis*, of course, could have been done only by taking numerous shortcuts, such as by foregoing the usual repairs and equipment checks. This would have added considerably to the risk of possibly stranding two crews in space. Such a risk would have been worthwhile, contends retired naval admiral Harold Gehman Jr., chairman of the CAIB. In the military, he pointed out, "We frequently launch 120 people to go save one," as there is an un-spoken contract with the people sent into harm's way. "NASA and the nation have that same contract with astronauts," Gehman says, "and it is my opinion, and from my personal background, that if there had been any erring, we would have erred on the side of taking the chance and going after them."[31]

Many space authorities remain unconvinced that a suc-cessful shuttle launch and in-space rescue could have been organized in time. This suggests that, although the astronauts were unaware of their fate, they were doomed as soon as the *Columbia* exited the Earth's atmosphere on January 16. As for-mer astronaut and space shuttle crew member Dick Covey said two days after the *Columbia* disaster, "If indeed we deter-mine that the foam that came off the external tank actually caused enough damage to have led to the catastrophe, yeah, I guess you could say we were watching a fatal launch when we saw it seventeen or eighteen days ago."[32]

The *Columbia* episode confirmed that when something goes wrong in space, the challenges rescuers face range from the difficult to the impossible. Of the handful of fatal accidents that have occurred in the history of human space exploration, all happened so quickly that ground controllers and emer-gency personnel barely had time to even get involved. In a number of other cases, however, dramatic rescues saved lives.

Losing *Liberty Bell 7*

The earliest space capsules the United States launched made parachute-assisted landings in the ocean. The capsules had a quick-release hatch that would allow an astronaut to escape if, for example, the craft—which was designed to float until res-cuers could come and pluck it from the water—started to sink.

On July 21, 1961, NASA was ready to launch the second American, Gus Grissom, into space aboard *Mercury 4*. Gris-som was familiar with risk, being a former test pilot who had flown combat missions during the Korean War, and was well aware of the numerous failures in previous unmanned launch tests. Just before launch, when a reporter said to him, "See you in a couple days," Grissom replied, "Yeah. I'll see you in a couple of days—or never."[33]

The quick, fifteen-minute flight from Cape Canaveral was not meant to achieve orbit. A successful parachute drop plopped Grissom and the capsule he had named *Liberty Bell 7*, because of its shape, into the Atlantic far off the coast of Florida. After about five minutes a Navy rescue helicopter piloted by James Lewis arrived to pick up the capsule with Grissom in it and deliver it to the deck of the aircraft carrier USS *Randolph*. According to author Paul Perry:

> The helicopter swung low over the capsule while Lt. John Reinhard, the co-pilot, prepared the helicopter's hook to snag a loop at the top of the capsule and pull it from the water. Just as the helicopter got into position, Lewis saw the spacecraft's escape hatch blow off its hinges and skip across the water. Right behind it was Grissom, escaping into the relative safety of the sea as water rushed into the sinking capsule.[34]

▼ A helicopter crewman lowers the recovery cable toward *Liberty Bell 7*, which proved to be too water-laden for retrieval.

RESCUING A SPACE RELIC

Liberty Bell 7 slowly succumbed to the forces of nature on the ocean floor for almost twenty-five years before maritime retrieval expert Curt Newport determined to salvage it. Newport was making a good living working at airplane crash salvage (and on the *Challenger* recovery), but he wanted to use his experience and knowledge, he has said, "to rewrite history." In the late 1980s, with finding the *Titanic* taken off the board by Robert Ballard's historic mission, Newport set his sights on the *Liberty Bell 7*. At a depth of more than three miles,

and not much bigger than the average sports utility vehicle, it would be a tough find. But Newport persisted for almost fifteen years before his team finally spotted it in April 1999 with a remotely operated undersea vehicle.

After successfully being brought to the surface, *Liberty Bell 7* has been lovingly restored to its former glory—its titanium skin was mostly unaffected by saltwater—and put on display to an appreciative public at the Kansas Cosmosphere and Space Center in Hutchison, Kansas.

▲ Restorer Greg Buckingham works on the *Liberty Bell 7* capsule after it was salvaged from the seafloor.

The spacecraft quickly began to take on water. Reinhard attached the cable, and the helicopter's engine strained to lift the capsule from the water. As the capsule became heavier and started to sink with each passing second, however, it pulled the helicopter toward the water. With three of the copter's landing wheels actually submerged, and in danger of being dragged into the water with the capsule, Lewis was forced to cut it loose. *Liberty Bell 7* sank sixteen thousand feet to the ocean floor, too deep for NASA to mount a recovery effort.

Pulled from the Drink

Meanwhile Grissom was struggling to stay afloat himself. As soon as he had landed in the capsule he had taken off his helmet and inserted a neck collar to make his space suit more watertight, just in case he had to make an emergency exit. The suit was now being tested by the elements, and was slowly losing the battle. An inlet valve Grissom had accidentally left open on his suit was admitting water. With one helicopter struggling with the capsule, a second was arriving to drop a line for the exhausted Grissom. Swells were beginning to sweep over Grissom's head as, just in the nick of time, he scrambled into the sling and the helicopter lifted him to safety.

Exactly what blew the hatch door out has never been determined. Grissom maintained he had not touched the trigger mechanism and that he was just lying there when the hatch self-detonated. Some NASA technicians have countered that this was not possible—extensive tests done both before and after the incident found no way it could accidentally blow. The issue could not be resolved even after an extensive undersea search located the *Liberty Bell 7* in 1999. The capsule—though not the telltale hatch door—has since been brought to the surface and restored.

The quick-release hatch was deemed dangerous and it was removed when the next generation craft, the Apollo series, was designed. Ironically, a quick-release hatch might have been able to save the life of Grissom and two fellow astronauts in the *Apollo 1* fire six years later.

Upside Down in a Frigid Lake

The Soviet space program also had a close call in the water that was even more harrowing than Grissom's experience. It occurred in October 1976, with Valerie Rozhdestvensky and

Vyacheslav Zudov onboard *Soyuz 23*. The mission was supposed to be a two-week rendezvous with *Salyut 5*, but the ground-controlled docking procedure failed. The cosmonauts, as first-timers in space, were not allowed to manually attempt the tricky maneuver. On their second day in space the capsule headed home.

The emergency night landing was a near disaster. The parachute opened successfully but the capsule crashed into the icy waters of Lake Tangiz. The wet parachute immediately sank and effectively anchored the craft in the middle of the lake. It also turned the capsule almost upside down, half in the water and half out. The cosmonauts could not open the escape hatch, which was underwater, because their space suits were too bulky and the in-rushing water would have prevented their getting out. It took them more than an hour just to take their space suits off in the cramped capsule. By then the cosmonauts were in danger of running out of oxygen, and the temperature inside their capsule was below 0° F. Even if they got out into the freezing water, their survival seemed unlikely unless rescuers could retrieve them within minutes. Helicopters and divers had arrived on scene but were hampered by windy, snowy weather, and the freezing water. Divers finally managed to attach a cable to the capsule, so the copter could drag the capsule ashore. According to Shayler:

> This was a rough ride for the two men inside, who were bruised and jostled as the experience further drained their strength as they finally reached dry ground. It took all their strength to open the manhole cover upper hatch, much to the surprise of the rescue crew, who had been expecting to find two frozen bodies inside.[35]

Zudov and Rozhdestvensky had spent almost ten hours inside the frigid capsule as it bobbed on the lake. Shayler notes that the Soviets have never officially confirmed reports that a number of rescuers died while saving the cosmonauts' lives.

"Houston, We've Had a Problem"

Rescues from frigid waters, and from capsules on the ground, are difficult but face known problems. Rescuing a crew whose craft develops problems in space is much more challenging. Space officials got an inkling of the potential difficulties when, en route to the Moon in April of 1970, *Apollo 13* experienced an oxygen tank explosion—visible from Earth, and felt as a jolt by the crew—that took out the spacecraft's main power supply. Astronaut Jim Lovell's announcement to ground control, "Okay Houston, we've had a problem here,"[36] turned out to be an understatement. The crisis deepened when, some fifteen minutes later, Lovell and fellow astronauts John Swigert and Fred Haise noticed oxygen gas from the only remaining oxygen tank venting into space.

The situation was grave. The oxygen tanks were crucial not only for power but also for the capsule's water and air supply. The "redundancy" of having two oxygen tanks was supposed to be a major safety factor, but NASA had never considered that both tanks might be compromised. Although mission control in Houston was initially reluctant to give up on the Moon landing, it soon became apparent that just getting the spacecraft safely back home was going to be a challenge. More than two days into the mission, *Apollo 13* was two hundred thousand miles from Earth and increasingly under the gravitational pull of the rapidly approaching Moon forty thousand miles away. Flight control faced a difficult choice:

▼ Artwork shows the *Apollo 13* command module explosion and the lunar module that astronauts used as a "lifeboat."

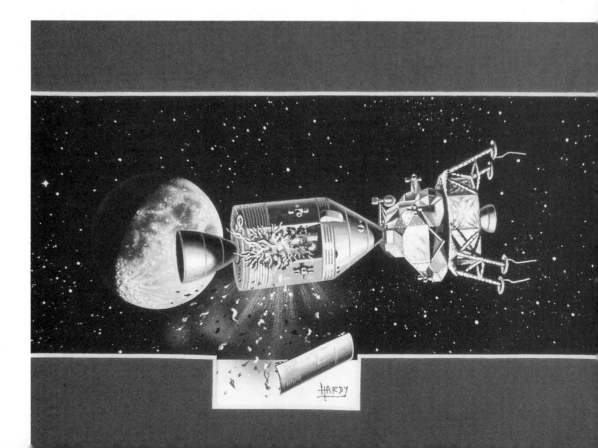

GENE KRANZ: FAILURE IS NOT AN OPTION

Made famous by actor Ed Harris's dead-on portrayal of him in the movie *Apollo 13*, Gene Kranz is an American original, a former test pilot turned NASA flight director. With experience that goes back to the Mercury and Gemini projects, Kranz literally wrote the procedure books for the successful Apollo lunar landings. Yet Kranz candidly admitted that many of the seemingly flawless missions to the Moon were in fact a series of hair-raising near misses. Upon learning of the *Apollo 13* explosion, NASA's initial fear was that it would lose three astronauts to an unanticipated technological failure, as had happened in the *Apollo 1* fire. In his 2000 book, *Failure Is Not an Option*, Kranz says:

> There was one big difference in this case. We could buy time.

What we could not accomplish through technology, or procedures and operating manuals, we might be able to manage by drawing on a priceless fund of experience, accumulated over almost a decade of sending men into places far beyond the envelope of Earth's protective, nurturing atmosphere. . . . These three astronauts were beyond our physical reach. But not beyond the reach of human imagination, inventiveness, and a creed that we all lived by: "Failure is not an option."

Kranz retired from NASA in 1994. Through his writings and speeches he is now a prominent spokesperson for human space exploration.

▲ Gene Kranz, smoking cigar, and NASA ground controllers are jubilant about the successful recovery of Lovell, on monitor, and the two other *Apollo 13* astronauts.

make a direct abort and jettison the lunar module, or keep the module and do a lunar flyaround to pick up the speed needed to return to Earth. The latter kept more options open but would take longer and put the craft out of touch with ground control for an agonizing two hours. The craft also had only half the battery power it would normally need for the trip home.

Over the next three days ground control and the trio of Apollo astronauts had to improvise a range of solutions to fast-dwindling supplies of electricity, air, and water. With the spacecraft's navigational system compromised by the explosion, they also had to devise a hands-on method to hit the atmosphere at just the right speed and angle. Flight director Gene Kranz was not optimistic. He called NASA deputy director of the Manned Spacecraft Center Chris Kraft, who was home taking a shower, and said, with some desperation, "Chris, you better get out here quick; I think we've had it!"[37] But Kranz famously refused to consider the possibility of mission failure and engaged his ground control coworkers in a desperate but inspired rescue mission.

Seat-of-the-Pants Space Control

The successful rescue of men and machine from near disaster was a triumph of teamwork and individual courage. The astronauts conserved battery power by moving from the command module into the lunar module, which was designed only for the short hop from lunar orbit to the surface of the Moon and back again. They powered down all nonvital functions, which meant they were soon working in a mostly dark and frigidly cold environment. They even shut down their onboard computer. With help from ground control, they improvised a device, which they called a "mailbox," from duct tape, plastic bags, and miscellaneous materials onboard to absorb carbon dioxide. The gas was threatening to build up to toxic levels within the lunar module.

It took both luck and skill to retrieve the crippled spacecraft. A tense moment came just before reentry, when the astronauts had to abandon the lunar module (which lacked a reentry heat shield) and return to the long-dormant command module. Fortunately, they succeeded in using the lunar module to repower the command module, a contingency that had never been tested. When the command module made a controlled de-orbit and finally landed safely in the Pacific, the

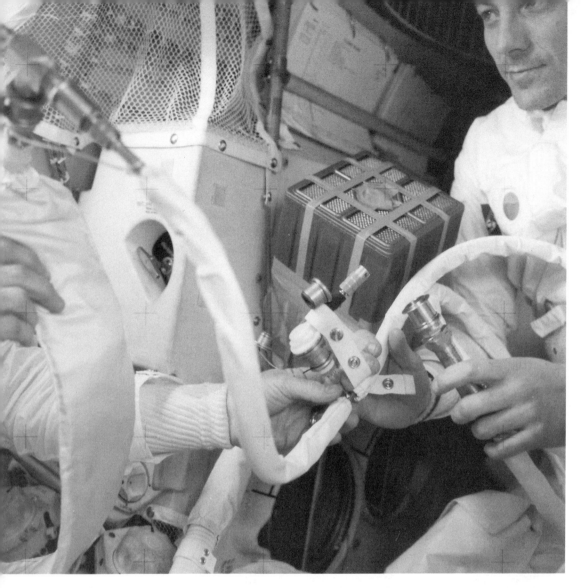

▲ Onboard *Apollo 13*, John Swigert helps to build an ad hoc device for absorbing carbon dioxide.

whole world was watching. The astronauts—and mission control—were hailed as heroes for their fearlessness in the face of tragedy.

Exploring Escape Options

Problems that develop on takeoff and landing, unlike those that happen in space, can be disastrous almost instantaneously and therefore are much more difficult rescue scenarios. Any emergency that causes a manned launch to be aborted represents a very risky scenario. Space programs try to have procedures and computer models in place to deal with such events, but the speeds and forces involved with rocket launches limit the options.

The first American space programs did have launchpad escape systems. For example, during countdown the Apollo capsules remained attached to an escape tower that could pull the capsule away from an exploding rocket. Lacking such options, the space shuttle program has always been vulnerable to launchpad explosions. From the point at which the orbiter separates from the solid rocket boosters, about two minutes after launch, to about nine minutes, it can detach from the external fuel tank and glide to an emergency landing site. There is also an escape pod, installed after the *Challenger* accident, which could be used within a few minutes of landing for low-altitude, low-speed emergencies. Certainly there were no escape options for the *Columbia* astronauts when the spacecraft disintegrated at 12,500 miles per hour upon reentry.

NASA's Aerospace Safety Advisory Panel (ASAP), composed of independent safety experts, pointed out the need for expanded crew escape systems on shuttle orbiters in each of its three annual reports prior to the *Columbia* disaster. In its 2002 report ASAP noted that crew safety guidelines that the agency developed in 1998 require escape systems for all flight vehicles but is not retroactive to the shuttle program.

Abort! Abort!

During the first two decades of its existence, the space shuttle program experienced only one launch disaster, the *Challenger* explosion. Six months earlier, on July 29, 1985, the *Challenger* had survived what has been the shuttle program's only so-called "abort to orbit." This occurred when one of the *Challenger*'s three main engines shut down about six minutes after launch. The spacecraft nevertheless achieved a 199-mile orbit and returned safely to Earth a week later.

A human spaceflight that had to be aborted before reaching orbit was the *Soyuz 18-A* launch in April 1975, whose two-man crew intended to dock with the *Salyut 4* space station. Five minutes after liftoff from Baikonur, things began to go wrong for cosmonauts Vasily Lazarev and Oleg Makarov. Vibrations in the spacecraft led to the premature firing of latches that linked the upper and lower rocket stages. One of the stages that was supposed to drop away and fall back to Earth clung instead to the spacebound craft, preventing it from reaching its intended orbit. The craft automatically aborted the mission at an altitude of about ninety miles. Lacking orbital speed, the separated descent

▲ Russian cosmonauts Makarov and Lazarev survived the perilous *Soyuz 18-A* pre-orbit abort.

module subjected the two cosmonauts to tremendous gravitational forces during the steep plunge through the atmosphere. They managed to survive the landing, and a rough roll partway down the side of a snowy mountain, with only minor injuries.

Both the U.S. and the Russian human spaceflight programs have long wrestled with the question of how best to deal with emergencies that develop on the launchpad or during the ascent to orbit. As space technology has developed since the 1970s, engineers have had to confront a new set of concerns relating to rescue from high-altitude-orbit space stations.

A Close Call Aboard *Mir*

Russian cosmonauts first occupied the *Mir* ("peace") space station in March 1986, about six weeks after the *Challenger* disaster. After a decade in space, however, it was increasingly plagued with problems that included power outages, loss of oxygen-generating and carbon-dioxide-scrubbing capacity, and cooling system leaks that put toxic substances into the craft's self-contained atmosphere. Any of these could have led to fatal consequences in space but were successfully managed. Still, the clear deterioration of the station—its original planned lifetime was only seven years—gave it a reputation as a tragedy-in-waiting during its final years.

On June 25, 1997, American astronaut Michael Foale and Russian cosmonauts Vasily Tsibliyev and Alexander Lazutkin were manning *Mir* as it circled more than two hundred miles above the Earth in the cold and remorseless void of space. Foale had been delivered to *Mir* a month earlier by an *Atlantis* docking, while the two Russians had been onboard *Mir* for much longer. The hectic schedule imposed by Russian ground control, as well as sleep experiments, had left the two Russians increasingly cranky and exhausted. They were also still stressed from a dangerous fire in February—an oxygen generator had burned out of control for fifteen minutes, filling the space station, as well as the Soyuz rescue vehicle, with smoke. The crew had not been able to put out the two-foot-long flames even with fire extinguishers. Instead they had to spray the hull to keep it from igniting, and wait for the fire to burn itself out. The two cosmonauts were also very concerned about the tricky docking procedure, with an unmanned *Progress* cargo craft.

A SOMBER PLAN FOR *APOLLO 11*

A memo only recently discovered in the U.S. National Archives details the grim emergency plan NASA had in place on July 20, 1969, when *Apollo 11* astronauts Neil Armstrong and Buzz Aldrin were the first humans to step on the Moon. They successfully landed in a lunar module while a third astronaut, Michael Collins, remained in the command module. Knowing that no rescue mission would have been possible, NASA had decided that if the astronauts were stranded on the lunar surface, communications with ground control would have been switched off. Armstrong and Aldrin would have been left to silent deaths, whether by natural cause or suicide. President Richard Nixon had prepared a speech telling the world, "For every human being who looks up at the moon in the nights to come will know that there is some corner of another world that is forever mankind." NASA officials apparently did not reveal any of these disaster plans to the astronauts.

Both the landing and the takeoff of the *Apollo 11* lunar module were considered risky at the time. The Moon landing was within seconds of having to be aborted, from dwindling fuel, when it successfully touched down.

Tsibliyev had to make a series of complex rocket firings, with timed accelerations and brakings, to control *Progress*'s approach. The television picture he received on a monitor onboard *Mir* turned out to be agonizingly fuzzy. Foale and Lazutkin peered out of various small windows but ended up not spotting the spacecraft until it was within about 150 yards of the space station, and closing fast. Tsibliyev kept his left pinky pinned to the control's braking lever but it was too late. *Progress* came flying up to the space station at three feet per second and crashed into it, damaging a solar array.

Abandon Module

Much more distressing to *Mir*'s three occupants, the impact also punched a hole in one of the station's six interlocking modules. Air started to hiss out into space. "It is the first decompression aboard an orbiting spacecraft in the history of manned space travel," Bryan Burrough notes in *Dragonfly*, his compelling history of NASA and *Mir*. Tsibliyev turned rigid with shock, Burrough says:

As Lazutkin hovers beside him, waiting for an order, Tsib-liyev remains at his post, staring dumbfounded at the screen, looking for all the world like the captain of some stricken celestial *Titanic*. "How can this be?" he asks. "How can this be?" After that his words are drowned out in the manic din of the master alarm.[38]

The exact location of the hole, and even which module was affected, was not clear to the astronauts during the first few frantic minutes of the emergency. With *Mir* depressuriz-ing, they faced a life-threatening crisis. When Lazutkin finally determined that the hole was in the Spektr module, he had to cut or tear apart some eighteen cables that snaked through a crucial hatchway before closing it. Sparks flew off one of the cables—a power cable—when he tried to cut it, alerting him to another problem: Sealing Spektr off from the rest of *Mir* was going to leave them dangerously low on power.

Lazutkin and Foale successfully sealed off Spektr, remov-ing the threat of total depressurization. In the ensuing days, with *Mir* operating on limited power, ground control began to make plans for a hazardous "internal space walk" to reconnect

▼ Solar panels and other *Mir* components are visible in this photo, taken from a docked *Atlantis*, a year before the *Progress* collision.

power cables to the three undamaged solar arrays. More problems ensued, however. During one training exercise a crew member inadvertently disconnected a cable that temporarily left the station without any power. When Tsibliyev developed an irregular heartbeat, repairs were postponed until the arrival of a replacement crew. It was not until early August that Russian cosmonauts did the internal space walk and reconnected eleven power cables. Despite a number of attempts, it proved very difficult to locate and patch the breach in Spektr's hull. The module was to remain depressurized and unused for the final forty-five months of *Mir's* life.

Like *Apollo 13*, this rescue was accomplished by a cooperative effort of crew members in space and ground controllers. The collision was a serious, near-fatal accident but the *Mir* space station also experienced an ongoing stream of problems, close calls, and mishaps that the Russians termed "*Mir*-haps." American astronauts became leery of going onboard and Russian cosmonauts became increasingly vocal in complaining about the unsafe conditions to Russian space officials. Finally, in late June 2000, the departure of the *Mir-28* crew left the space station permanently abandoned. Nine months later, Russian ground controllers guided *Mir* into a final suicide dive. Observers in parts of the southern Pacific saw *Mir* disintegrate in a streak across the night sky. Few space enthusiasts mourned the loss of what was widely regarded during its last years as a rickety, accident-prone craft. But it cannot be denied that *Mir* spent more than fifteen years in space, and, despite a number of close calls, all of its visitors survived to return to Earth alive.

Limited Options

During its final years, *Mir* played a major role in setting up its replacement in orbit, the *International Space Station* (*ISS*). This spacecraft began permanent occupation in November 2000 and has grown, with the addition of modules, to the size of a three-bedroom house. Though more advanced, and presumably safer, than *Mir*, if something were to go disastrously wrong aboard the *ISS*, ground-based options would be limited. The near future may well see the need for challenging rescues onboard the *ISS*.

CHAPTER FOUR

Challenging Investigations

Many of the people of Texas were not even aware that the *Columbia* was aloft when they heard an ominous roar coming from the west early that Saturday morning. Within minutes they began to have firsthand experiences, close encounters of an unwanted kind, with the *Columbia*, as pieces of it rained down on their fields and streets and yards. Government investigators emphasized the need to report these findings, and to not disturb them. Collecting and analyzing this debris is one of the most important first steps in investigating space tragedies like the loss of the *Columbia*. Such investigations often involve thousands of people, cost tens of millions of dollars, and take months to complete because of the many challenges they face.

Finding the Root Cause

Space accident investigations look for both the immediate symptom or problem—the physical or mechanical event that touched off the disaster—and for the root, or ultimate, cause. The root cause often includes command decisions, the organizational climate, and the contractor relationships that contributed to the disaster scenario. Critics of NASA have charged that the agency too often takes an engineering approach to problems by focusing on fixing faulty technology. If deep-seated organizational factors are ignored, the correction may not be permanent.

For example, the investigation into the *Apollo 1* fire that killed three astronauts never did identify the specific short circuit, electric arc, or other wiring problem that caused the inferno. What it did identify were the half dozen conditions

and oversights that made the
These included the sealed cabin
atmosphere; the many combust
vulnerable wiring carrying space
provisions for the crew to escape
ical assistance.

Beyond identifying these h
vestigators also addressed the
tions came to exist. Among th
Apollo team failed to give adeq
dane b
crew sa
reveale
and e
quality

In
port
on th
dent
as the
and s
tions
fault
vote
cau
in h

AN ANNUAL SAFETY REVIEW

One of the effects of the *Apollo 1* disaster was that Congress established the Aerospace Safety Advisory Panel. ASAP is made up of nine independent safety experts, each appointed by the NASA administrator for a six-year term. The panel produces an annual report that it submits to both Congress and NASA, and releases publicly. The report highlights both the good things NASA is doing to improve its safety record and the areas it needs improvement on.

In its *Annual Report for 2002*, which was completed before the *Columbia* accident, the panel commended NASA for, among others, overall safety and *International Space Station* operations. One area of concern it noted was NASA's unwillingness to commit to a program for adding crew escape systems to the space shuttle orbiters. Another issue that the panel felt NASA needed to make better progress on was proactively reviewing the shuttle's critical ground and flight systems, which ASAP said were showing signs of wearing out due to age and use.

ten oam insulation that broke
red tted that was one area of
sch investigation would be
recss virtually all aspects of
pr
ag
pe
p **ris Field**
c an altitude of two hun-
t e than twelve thousand
t wreckage were strewn
nited States. Since the
an provide prominent
—of a failure, this huge
e to investigators, in-
ordoned off from the

▲ I
NAS
rock
like t
durin
launc

▲
se
pe
lu
ea

and dogged ground searching allowed recovery teams to locate large pieces of the craft such as a landing gear as well as smaller items such as a helmet, a laptop computer, and thermal tiles. Saddened ground searchers also found body parts.

Hazards on the Ground

The parts of the demolished *Columbia* that fell to Earth were crucial pieces of evidence for the accident investigation. They also represented a potential hazard to people on the ground, both before and after impact. Some of the falling debris chunks were quite large, such as the five-hundred-pound nose cone that burrowed into the ground near Hemphill, Texas. Authorities estimated that another large piece of debris, a seven-hundred-pound engine part that came down in Louisiana's Kisatchie National Forest, hit the ground while traveling at least two hundred miles per hour.

Some debris posed further hazards on the ground. Certain shuttle parts, such as hatches, are fitted with explosive bolts that could seriously injure someone who mishandled them. The shuttles also carry toxic fuels. NASA officials warned the public not to touch debris because of these dangers. Although there were a number of reports of people taking shuttle parts as souvenirs, in the end no one on the ground was injured from the *Columbia* tragedy. (Two searchers did die in a helicopter accident.)

A Giant Jigsaw Puzzle

All of the recovered *Columbia* debris was collected in a huge hangar at the Kennedy Space Center. A model of the orbiter was painted on the floor and debris pieces were distributed to their approximate locations. Four months after the accident the hangar held more than seventy thousand items. The pieces weighed almost eighty thousand pounds, representing more than one-third of the *Columbia* by weight.

BEWARE BELOW

The two largest spacecraft to reenter the Earth's atmosphere were the 130-ton Russian *Mir* in March 2001 and the seventy-ton American *Skylab* in July 1979. Some of the forty tons of *Mir* debris that survived burn-up were automobile-sized chunks that splashed harmlessly into the Pacific Ocean, somewhere between New Zealand and Chile. *Skylab*'s self-destruction, which unlike *Mir*'s was uncontrolled, happened partially over a remote area of coastal Australia. No one was hurt by fragments as large as a one-ton oxygen tank. A U.S. State Department official who visited the area six days later was given a $400 ticket for littering.

▲ A hangar at the Kennedy Space Center contains recovered pieces of the *Columbia* laid out in relative positions.

Accident investigators used a number of methods to try to identify pieces of debris and painstakingly put them back together. Most of the parts, including all of the thermal tiles, have unique identifying numbers on them. Parts that were partially damaged or burned could sometimes be matched using one-to-one scale engineering drawings. This same process of reconstruction had been used after the *Challenger* accident in 1986. It takes many months but can yield important clues about the cause of the tragedy.

Elusive Independent Experts

The *Challenger* investigation also provided a model for assembling a top-notch team of independent experts. In the wake of the *Challenger* accident, NASA had formed a team of NASA employees to conduct an internal analysis of what happened. It was not long, however, before critics of NASA in Congress and elsewhere complained that the agency should not be left to investigate itself. President Ronald Reagan thus appointed an independent investigative commission headed by former secretary of state William Rogers. It eventually included astronauts Neil Armstrong and Sally Ride, test pilot Chuck Yeager, and Nobel Prize-winning scientist Richard

Feynman. Congressional committees also probed the *Challenger* accident. The process prompted NASA to establish protocols relating to the need for an independent investigative committee after any future space disasters.

Within hours of the *Columbia* accident, therefore, NASA administrator Sean O'Keefe had begun to organize both an in-house agency investigation and the independent committee that became the Columbia Accident Investigation Board. His first set of appointments for the latter soon drew congressional scrutiny. The choice of Harold Gehman as chair was logical, given his experience cochairing the 2000 investigation into the terrorist attack on the USS *Cole* off the coast of Yemen. Four of O'Keefe's other six appointments, however, were also either current or retired military figures. NASA has long had close ties to the U.S. military, both in terms of projects (launching military satellites, for example) and personnel (O'Keefe himself is a former secretary of the Navy). NASA officials note that most experts in highly technical and specialized fields relevant to space accident investigations almost inevitably already have some relationship with either NASA or with space/military contractors.

▼ A Columbia Accident Investigation Board reconstruction technician matches debris pieces from the destroyed orbiter.

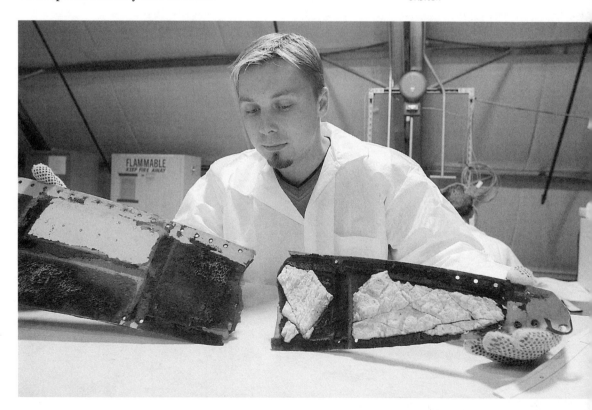

Some members of Congress questioned the lack of civilian representatives on the CAIB. They also soon objected to some of the procedural guidelines NASA was imposing on the independent committee. These included a sixty-day deadline for submitting a final written report, and the fact that the report would be submitted to NASA rather than being immediately released to the public. By mid-February O'Keefe had responded to the criticisms by making an additional half dozen appointments, including Ride, Stanford University physics professor Douglas Osheroff, and Space Policy Institute director John Logsdon. O'Keefe also withdrew the sixty-day deadline and agreed that the report would be publicly available.

In his first public statements Gehman was adamant that his committee's investigation would be independent, especially from NASA. "There's only one investigation going on," he said, "and that's our investigation."[40] He promised to pull no punches in questioning top NASA and industry officials, and he encouraged any NASA "whistle-blowers" (workers with inside knowledge of wrongdoing) to come forward.

▼ CAIB member Stephen Turcotte examines an actual panel from the leading edge of an orbiter wing.

The CAIB and other government investigations sought out world-class experts from such fields as aerodynamics, vehicle structures and materials, accident reconstruction, and thermal properties. The investigative committees interviewed experts, held public meetings and press conferences, and pored over evidence relating to materials, operations, and technology. They paid close attention to the data available from the *Columbia's* last minutes.

Telltale Clues from the Black Box

Much like large commercial airplanes, spacecraft have an on-board black box, capable of recording vital flight data and remaining intact after a crash. The *Columbia's* black box was located in eastern Texas more than six weeks after the crash. It was designed to provide information on liftoff and reentry, especially with regard to factors such as aerodynamic pressure, temperature, and vibrations. NASA officials feared that the extreme temperatures of atmospheric breakup were enough to erase the recorder's data, but upon analysis the box offered up useful information, including several seconds from the very end of *Columbia's* flight—data from after the point at which ground control had lost contact with the shuttle.

The information provided useful clues for the investigation. Temperature data sensors showed that the *Columbia's* wing began to heat up about four minutes and thirty seconds after reentry, rather than the eight minutes previously thought. This finding lent support to the theory that the leading edge of *Columbia's* left wing had, not a small crack, but rather perhaps a soccer-ball-sized hole, most likely caused by being struck on takeoff by a piece of insulation foam off of the external fuel tank. The hole, thought to be where third-of-an-inch-thick reinforced carbon panels join the leading wing edge to the thermal tiles on the orbiter's underbody, would have allowed super-hot gases to rush into the empty space behind the panels. This could have quickly destroyed the wing and led to the breakup of the shuttle.

As useful as the black box was in the *Columbia* investigation, space officials looking into a disaster also have access to extensive mission control-collected data. Files and files of data were beamed directly from countless parts of the spacecraft to ground-control computers. In both the *Challenger*

▲ NASA mission evaluators pore over data as they reconstruct the sequence of events leading up to the *Challenger* tragedy.

and *Columbia* disasters, investigators immediately began analyzing this data for clues about what might have gone wrong aboard the orbiters.

Reconstructing the *Columbia* Accident

The *Columbia* investigation gradually closed in on the very first suspect: the piece of foam that struck the left wing upon takeoff. This incident was noted as potentially worrisome from day one, sixteen days before the accident. The one-page "mission evaluation room" report filed after liftoff on January 16, 2003, by NASA official Don L. McCormack Jr. contained the following paragraph:

> At approximately 81 seconds mission elapsed time, a large light-colored piece of debris was seen to originate from an area near the [External Tank]/Orbiter forward attach bipod. The debris appeared to move outboard and then fall aft along the left side of the Orbiter fuselage, striking the leading edge of the left wing. The strike appears to have oc-

curred on or relatively close to the wing glove near the Orbiter fuselage. After striking the left wing the debris broke into a spray of white-colored particles that fell aft along the underside of the Orbiter left wing. The spray of particles was last seen near the left Solid Rocket Booster exhaust plume. Further screening of the high speed and high-resolution long-range tracking films that may show more detail of this event will begin this morning.[41]

This report prompted NASA to request the debris impact analysis from subcontractor Boeing. By January 21, five days after liftoff, Boeing had run its computer models and determined that the foam would not present a safety concern for the orbiter. Even after February 1, when the *Columbia* disintegrated on reentry, NASA officials seemed confident that the foam could not have been the culprit. On February 12, NASA Administrator Sean O'Keefe said the foam impact was "the functional equivalent . . . of a Styrofoam cooler blowing off a pickup truck ahead of you on the highway."[42] From early in its investigation, the CAIB decided to challenge NASA's ready dismissal of the foam incident. The board arranged for a much more thorough series of debris impact tests at a contractor lab in San Antonio, Texas.

From May to July 2003, engineers conducted seven impact tests using a huge nitrogen-powered gun to shoot pieces of insulation foam at speeds of more than five hundred miles per hour. Targets included thermal tiles, the reinforced carbon panels found on the leading edge of orbiters' wings, and various other materials. A number of these tests showed that a speeding piece of foam like the one that fell off of the shuttle's external tank could indeed cause what the CAIB called "visible and significant damage"[43] to wing panels or to the T-seals that hold them together. In some cases cracks or gaps were one-quarter-inch wide by

A MORE OPEN AND ACCOMMODATING NASA?

After the *Challenger* disaster in 1986, NASA was widely criticized for how it handled the investigation. Reporters charged that NASA officials misled the press, thwarted outside investigators, and even shredded documents to cover up its poor safety record. In the first week after the *Columbia* accident, the difference was "night and day," according to one commentator, as NASA held frank briefings, shared data, and even showed emotions. "Instead of stonewalling reporters," noted *Boston Globe* media reporter Mark Jurkowitz, "the agency holds two news briefings a day—emanating from Washington and from Houston—and its officials are widely viewed as being candid and even remorseful." The pre-*Challenger* managers who viewed the space program as infallible, Jurkowitz says, have been replaced by officials "better prepared to handle a human, scientific, and public relations emergency."

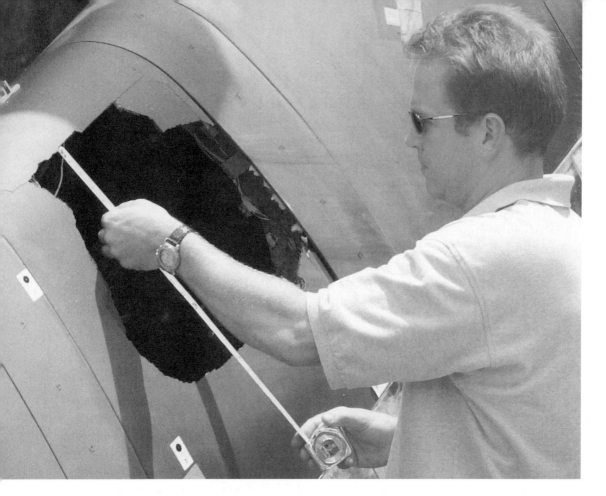

▲ The final foam impact test left a gaping hole in a wing panel, similar to (though probably slightly larger than) the hole thought to have doomed the *Columbia*.

almost two feet long, big enough to allow explosively hot gas into the interior of the wing during reentry.

The final test was the most dramatic, with a foam chunk punching a gaping, sixteen-inch-wide hole in an actual wing panel removed from the *Atlantis*. The impact also dislodged an adjoining T-seal and left a maze of cracks in the damaged panel. "We have found the smoking gun,"[44] claimed Scott Hubbard, a high-ranking NASA official and member of the CAIB. This was no Styrofoam cooler hitting the *Columbia*'s wing, Hubbard noted, likening it instead to "a 70-pound sack of cement hitting the front of a car traveling 60 miles per hour."[45] The board noted that the earlier Boeing tests had gone wrong by greatly overestimating, without any real data, the strength of the carbon panels.

"A Gaping Hole in NASA's Safety Culture"

The results of the foam impact tests established what the CAIB said was a compelling link between the liftoff incident and the damage to the left wing that led to the *Columbia*'s destruction. The CAIB noted that equally as important as the direct physical cause of the accident were flaws in NASA's management and in its approach to dealing with safety system failures. The board was highly critical of NASA's actions and decisions while the *Columbia* was on its last mission. The final foam impact test, commented space analyst James Oberg, "that left a gaping hole in a simulated space shuttle wing also graphically unveiled the gaping hole in NASA's safety culture."[46]

The CAIB observed that within the first few days of *Columbia*'s last mission a number of NASA engineers repeatedly suggested that U.S. spy satellites be asked to photograph the suspected wing damage. This was possible, and in fact may well have revealed the damage. NASA mission managers, however, nixed the request, at least in part because they believed that, if the wing was damaged, there was nothing that could be done to save the crew. The CAIB came to regard as fundamentally wrong this unwillingness to explore options. Although the wing hole was probably too large to repair in space, the CAIB faulted NASA for not even considering the possibility of launching the *Atlantis* on a rescue mission.

The CAIB also pointed out that at least seven foam fragments had hit orbiters during previous launches. Exactly why the external tank was shedding foam remains unclear.

SPACE SLEUTH JAMES OBERG

One of the world's most prominent authorities on human spaceflight and space accidents is former space engineer James Oberg. Over the past decade he has parlayed his twenty-two years of experience working as a mission controller and space shuttle designer at NASA's Johnson Space Center in Houston into a thriving writing and consulting enterprise. Oberg has developed a depth of knowledge not only on the American but also the Russian space program, which he has written about in a number of his ten books, including *Red Star in Orbit* and *Uncovering Soviet Disasters*.

A common theme in Oberg's work relates to how easy it is to understand many space disasters, from *Apollo 1* to *Columbia*, in hindsight, since errors in judgment so often play a critical role. Oberg says on his website that one of his goals is to "help develop a 'pre-hindsight' that allows aerospace workers to 'see the future as if the accident had already happened,' and thus develop timely tactics to avoid catastrophe as often as 'humanly possible.'"

Weakness in the spray-on insulation has been attributed to everything from woodpeckers (which drilled holes in it) to hail. The main factor may simply be the extremes in temperature the foam is exposed to—the liquid fuels put into the external tank reach super-cold temperatures of −400° F.

More important than the question of why foam was falling onto the orbiters was the question of why NASA had not more effectively predicted the possibility of disaster, and then dealt with the problem. NASA officials admitted that the apparent lack of consequences from foam failures led them to view the foam-shedding as primarily a maintenance, rather than a safety, issue. "Each time it ran a risk and succeeded, the institution learned the wrong lesson," University of Pennsylvania sociologist Charles Bosk noted. "Instead of saying, 'I was lucky,' you say, 'Maybe that wasn't so risky after all.'"[47]

NASA's shortcomings in foreseeing the *Columbia* disaster and the agency's misjudgments during the final flight were criticized in the CAIB's scathing, 248-page final report, issued on August 26, 2003. The report documented pervasive safety lapses at NASA and called for sweeping reforms. Among the twenty-nine specific recommendations were fifteen that the board believed should be required before any future shuttle launch. For example, the report recommended that NASA upgrade its launch imaging systems to provide at least three useful views of the shuttle from liftoff to solid rocket separation; that the agency use the federal government's orbital spy satellites to photograph every shuttle in space; and that NASA adopt a shuttle flight schedule consistent with available resources.

Sharing Investigation Results

The CAIB's investigation no doubt piqued the interest of other space agencies in addition to NASA. Space exploration has become an international affair in the past decade, with the European Space Agency becoming increasingly active in launching satellites and developing aerospace technology. Investigations into human space tragedies, as well as into commercial disasters (like losing a half-billion-dollar satellite in a launchpad explosion), can help avoid repeats of the same mistake in the future. On at least a few occasions, keeping the results of a space accident officially secret has hindered the advance of knowledge and arguably contributed to a similar, very preventable accident.

◀ Russian cosmonaut-in-training Valentin Bondarenko died in circumstances similar to those that later killed the *Apollo 1* astronauts.

Perhaps the most prominent example of how candor could have saved lives occurred in the Soviet Union in March 1961. Twenty-five-year-old cosmonaut-in-training Valentin Bondarenko was inside an oxygen-enriched pressure chamber on the ground when he accidentally discarded some small, alcohol-soaked cotton swabs onto an electric hot plate. The inside of the chamber ignited in a flash. Bondarenko was burned so badly by the time rescuers could free him that he died eight hours later. The Soviet investigation quickly identified the danger of training in an oxygen chamber but kept its findings secret. It was not until 1986, during the period of glasnost (public openness), before a Soviet book or magazine identified Bondarenko as one of the first persons to die during spaceflight training. If U.S. space engineers had known of the cause of his death, the fatal *Apollo 1* fire, which occurred six years later and was similar in many respects, might never have happened.

The need for greater openness between the American and Soviet space programs about accident investigations became more urgent during the 1970s. This was because, as a demonstration of the new détente (relaxation of tensions) between the two countries, a space docking between Apollo and Soyuz capsules was planned. The Americans still had reservations, however, about the safety of the Soyuz capsules, since they had received conflicting information about the cause of the depressurization disaster that killed the three *Soyuz 11* cosmonauts. As a result, in 1974 the Soviets appointed Professor K.D. Bushuyev to make a presentation to the Americans about the accident and the steps that the Soviet space program had taken to make certain that it could not recur. Bushuyev's detailed report on the exact sequence of failures that led to the fatal cabin depressurization reassured the Americans and led the way to a successful Apollo-Soyuz docking on July 15, 1975. According to a NASA history of the Apollo-Soyuz project:

> This presentation on *Soyuz 11* and the fact that the Professor had been able to release the exact details, even though it did not immediately affect the safety of the American crew, was an important step forward in forging a partnership. Both sides had to establish faith in the other's hardware and believe that it was safe. The Soviets had opened up and talked about an extremely painful subject. It had taken two years for them to do so, but the resulting level of candor . . . indicated that both sides were reaching the level of trust necessary to build a genuine space partnership.[48]

This space partnership grew even stronger over the next two decades, as numerous cooperative ventures were accomplished on *Mir* and then on the *International Space Station*. The spirit of cooperation probably saved a number of lives and remains an important component of efforts to prevent space disasters.

CHAPTER FIVE

Preventing Future Accidents

Virtually every mission into space has experienced some safety related incidents. With space agencies now selling space station trips to wealthy tourists to cover costs (California investment fund manager Dennis Tito became the first space tourist in April 2001 when *Soyuz TM-32* delivered him to the *International Space Station*), engineers and safety experts worldwide are under increasing pressure to constantly review goals and practices in an effort to prevent future catastrophes.

The nature of space technology continues to determine what can and cannot be done to reduce the risks of going into space. Rockets remain necessary to escape the Earth's gravitational pull, airtight capsules to survive in space, and some sort of heat-deflection technology to return to Earth without burning up.

Famous Launchpad Disasters

The Chinese were shooting off small rockets at least seven hundred years ago but the history of space rocketry is really only a century old. It was in 1903 that Konstantin Tsiolkovsky, an obscure Russian schoolteacher, worked out the theoretical underpinnings of reaching space with rockets, including the need for liquid fuel and multiple booster stages. The other two major twentieth-century pioneers of rocketry were the American scientist Robert Goddard, who launched the first successful liquid-propelled rocket in Auburn, Massachusetts, on March 16, 1926 (it flew about 150 feet), and German-born Wernher von Braun. In March 1942 a team of German scientists and engineers led by von Braun inaugurated the space age with the launch of the unmanned V2. Though used as a weapon, the V2 was the first rocket capable of reaching space.

Rocket technology has improved vastly since the pioneering days of Goddard and von Braun but rockets still explode with surprising regularity. A mid-1990s "space systems failure review" of the four previous decades identified a total of 163 major launch vehicle failures or malfunctions, although admittedly most of these occurred during the first fifteen years of space exploration. Because satellite and research rockets are unmanned, and most rocket explosions occur after liftoff, injuries and deaths on the ground are rare. Other than the *Challenger*, the only rocket-related fatality in the United States was in September 1990 when part of a rocket fell from a crane and exploded at Edwards Air Force Base in California, killing one person. The Soviet Union, on the other hand, has

▼ Rocket launches, like this July 1950 Cape Canaveral shot, are inherently dangerous.

ROCKET-FIGHTER CLAIMS LIFE OF FIRST PILOT

As Allied forces closed in on an increasingly desperate Germany at the end of World War II, the Germans began to test a radical new rocket-powered fighter. The Bachem (after designer Erich Bachem) Ba 349 Natter ("viper") had stubby wooden wings, a one-person cockpit, and four solid-fuel rocket motors attached to its twenty-foot-long fuselage. Shot straight into the sky from a vertical tower with guide rails, the Natter was supposed to come rapidly up under its bomber target and release its missiles. The pilot would then eject and parachute to safety. The rocket-plane would be destroyed on impact but the Germans would recover and reuse the rocket motors.

On February 28, 1945, the Germans tested the Natter in the world's first vertically launched, manned rocket flight. When the interceptor reached an altitude of sixteen hundred feet, the canopy flew off. The rocket-plane rolled over on its back and plunged into the ground, killing test pilot Lothar Siebert, who may have been hit by the canopy. German pilots managed to survive a few Natter tests over the next month but the machine never saw combat. German forces destroyed most Natters to prevent Allied forces from capturing them. Only two Natters still exist, one in Germany and one at the Smithsonian's National Air and Space Museum in Washington, D.C.

experienced at least two major launchpad disasters in which scores of people lost their lives.

The single most deadly rocket explosion occurred in 1960 at the Soviet test range in Tyuratam. Marshall Mitrofan Nedelin, commander of the Russian strategic missile forces, rushed the launch of a newly developed missile in spite of numerous unresolved technical problems. On the launchpad problems multiplied, including a fuel leak, electrical failures, and valve malfunctions. Postponed overnight, the launch became even more urgent. By then technicians were making repairs and adjustments to the fully fueled, ready-to-fire rocket, an invitation to disaster. Sure enough, a key control was prematurely turned, firing the rocket's second stage. Fuel in the first stage exploded in a fireball that engulfed upwards of one hundred people within one hundred yards, including Nedelin. According to RussianSpaceWeb.com:

> Probably, many people were incinerated instantly, while many others died in the following several seconds of a living hell. Eyewitnesses described a horrifying scene of burning people running from the rocket or hanging on their safety harnesses from the access pads. Those who

were on the ground and tried to escape the flames had to overcome the fence surrounding the pad and a fresh tar, which was melting under their feet. Some had no choice but to jump into the wells dug around the launch complex, only to suffocate from the poisonous propellant fumes released by the inferno.[49]

The Soviet government announced that Nedelin and ninety-one others had died in an airplane crash. It was not until 1989 that the Soviets allowed publication of a magazine article on the launchpad explosion, which is now thought to have claimed more than 130 lives.

An almost equally disastrous Soviet rocket disaster occurred on March 18, 1980, at the Plesetsk launch complex. Two hours before a Soviet Vostok ("east") rocket was scheduled to be launched, soldiers discovered an oxygen leak in a pipeline close to the booster. Under pressure from officials to maintain the schedule, engineers decided to improvise a temporary fix using a wet rag taken from a nearby truck. Unfortunately the rag bore traces of oil and gas and quickly caught on fire. Within a minute the entire launchpad and then the booster itself was ablaze. When it finally exploded on its launchpad, the rocket killed fifty people.

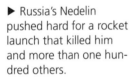
▶ Russia's Nedelin pushed hard for a rocket launch that killed him and more than one hundred others.

Rocketing into the Future

Powerful rockets are necessary to launch craft into space but are inherently dangerous. Some advances have been made to make rocketry safer. These include technical improvements in guidance systems and computerized control. Identifying software errors is a major concern, as these have led to a number of near disasters involving both launch rockets and orbital maneuvering rockets. "In 1988," Oberg notes, "a confused guidance computer nearly jettisoned the *Soyuz T-M5*'s rocket engine section while the crew was still in orbit, a malfunction that would have doomed the men to a slow death by suffocation. Only the alertness of one of the pilots detected and aborted the insane command."[50] A 1997 Soyuz mission also almost ended in catastrophe when a computer fired the wrong control rockets on a jettisoned module, directing it on a collision course for the manned capsule.

The next generation of rocket technology may lead to safer launches. One of the most promising new concepts is being developed by Kelly Space and Technology of San Bernardino, California. Its idea is to have a Boeing 747 tow an "Astroliner," a reusable launch vehicle similar to but somewhat smaller than a shuttle orbiter, off of a conventional runway and up to a launch altitude of twenty thousand feet. From there a two-stage rocket system would blast the *Astroliner* into orbit, with the larger, and more expensive, first stage being fully reusable. Kelly officials note that tow-launching has a proven history of safety and reliability. They also contend that having the first stage ignite at altitude can result in unprecedented cost savings, additions to payload capacity, and reductions in the weight of reentry insulation.

Given the difficulty of making rockets safer, space engineers have long debated whether manned launches should be provided with escape capsules for the crew. If the monetary cost were the only consideration, the choice might be straightforward. But the necessary additional equipment adds to overall weight and complexity, and thus comes with its own set of risks.

When an Escape Capsule Worked

On September 26, 1983, a Soviet Soyuz launch vehicle containing cosmonauts Vladimir Titov and Gennadi Strekalov was prepared to relieve the crew on *Salyut 7*. Less than two minutes before the planned launch, however, a fuel spill caused the rocket booster to catch on fire. Launch control quickly made the decision to abort the countdown and to activate an escape system that Soviet engineers had designed in case of just such an emergency. The capsule was shot away from the top of the launch rocket, at extremely high g (gravitational) forces—zero to seven hundred miles per hour in

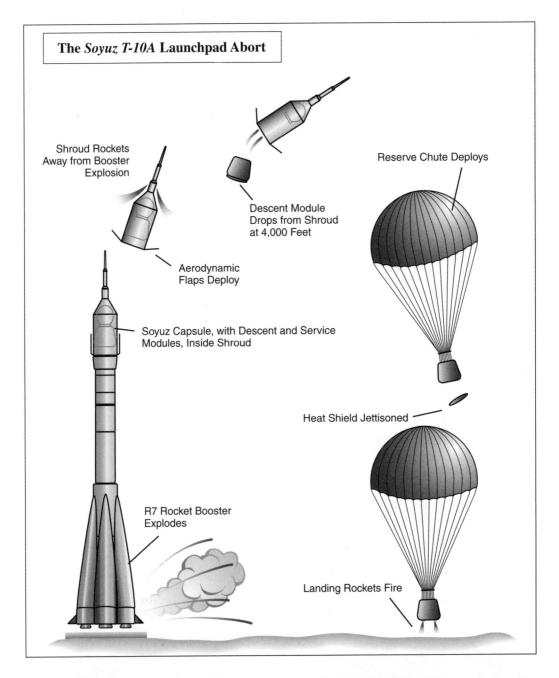

The *Soyuz T-10A* Launchpad Abort

Shroud Rockets Away from Booster Explosion

Descent Module Drops from Shroud at 4,000 Feet

Reserve Chute Deploys

Aerodynamic Flaps Deploy

Soyuz Capsule, with Descent and Service Modules, Inside Shroud

Heat Shield Jettisoned

R7 Rocket Booster Explodes

Landing Rockets Fire

three seconds—inside a shroud that formed the rocket nose. Within a matter of seconds after the top of the rocket was projected away, the fuel-filled booster exploded, completely destroying the launch complex.

At an altitude of about four thousand feet, the capsule was released out of the bottom of the protective shroud and started to plummet to the ground. In quick succession the capsule successfully deployed its quick-opening reserve parachute (it was too close to the ground for the main chutes) and discarded its heat shield. Just before impact it briefly fired its landing rockets. Even so the landing, more than two miles distant from the fiery launchpad, was rough. Titov and Strekalov were bruised but glad to be alive, especially considering that the abort system had never been fully tested—it was considered too risky.

One Soviet official later admitted that this was "a very serious accident . . . just six seconds from a Soviet *Challenger*!"[51] *Soyuz T-10A* was the only such instance of using an escape capsule to make a manned off-the-pad abort, and, as of mid-2003, the last failed attempt to reach a space station. Similar launchpad escape mechanisms have been considered for the space shuttle but, so far, not installed.

Repairs in Space: A Risky Idea

Space engineers have long had to deal with the paradox that adding a safety feature can improve one system but actually increase the level of risk elsewhere in the program. A rocket that is made heavier and sturdier, for example, thereby needs more fuel to achieve orbit. Similarly, there are inherent risks to carrying extra fuel, oxygen, and food to increase the safety cushion for emergency action. The issue of making repairs in space, especially when using space walks and docking maneuvers, represents another difficult balancing act that space programs face as they attempt to prevent accidents.

After the *Columbia* disaster, space experts revived the issue of whether a reentry disaster could be prevented if crew members could identify and fix damage to the exterior of the craft. In the early days of the space shuttle program, NASA did consider, for example, having a tile repair kit onboard each mission. The idea was abandoned, however, after NASA engineers determined that astronauts would be as likely to damage sound tiles—by bumping up against them or by hitting them with a remote arm—as they would be to repair a broken one.

▲ A cloud-covered Earth serves as the backdrop as untethered astronaut Mark Lee tests a new space walk rescue system in September 1994.

Similar considerations must go into any option that involves a space walk, which is an inherently risky endeavor. In the total vacuum of space, a technical glitch—or impact with a tiny piece of space debris—that resulted in loss of space suit pressure would result in almost instant death. Extremes of temperature in space are another challenge. Since the difference between shadow and full sunlight in space can be more than 400° F, a failure in the suit's sophisticated heat-regulation system can be disastrous. Spacewalking astronauts have experienced both cold fingers and, after a rip in an outer layer of a space suit, sunburn.

Space walkers must also go through elaborate pre- and post-walk routines to avoid the bends, the same disorder that is sometimes fatal to deep-sea divers. (The cause is the release of nitrogen gas bubbles in bodily tissue, from a rapid decrease in air pressure after being in a compressed atmosphere.) Space suits are now typically kept at a pressure that is about one-third of what is normal on the surface of the Earth because too much pressure prevents normal movements. "If the suit pressure was higher," space writer Lydia Dotto notes, "it would be like trying to work inside an inflated balloon."[52]

Keeping the Streak Going

Space walks so far have come off without major problems, though there have been numerous close calls, starting with the very first space walk in history when the Russian cosmonaut Alexei Leonov had trouble fitting back into the depressurization chamber. In February 2001, American astronaut Robert Curbeam was spacewalking at the *International Space Station* to make a repair on the station's cooling system. One of the lines sprang a leak, spraying ammonia into space. Curbeam was enveloped in a cloud of the frozen crystals. Ammonia is toxic enough to be potentially deadly, and Curbeam had to put his space suit through a difficult decontamination process, with the help of fellow astronaut Tom Jones.

After two astronauts at the *International Space Station* made the one-hundredth space walk in NASA's history in February 2001, veteran spacewalker Michael Lopez-Alegria noted that it was a small miracle that no lives had yet been lost, given the risks involved and the increasing need for space walks to build and repair the *ISS*. "We have to keep our fingers crossed," Lopez-Alegria told Space.com. "It's kind of like an undefeated team. The streak can only go on for so long. But so far, so good."[53]

AN ABANDONED LIFEBOAT

For much of the 1990s NASA developed and tested a thirty-foot-long, eight-ton mini-orbiter that would land on Earth under a huge parasail. Dubbed the *X-38 CRV* (crew return vehicle), its main function would be to serve as an emergency rescue vehicle that could return up to seven astronauts from the *International Space Station* in case of an emergency. (The *ISS* currently cannot be occupied by more than three astronauts, the limit of the Soyuz return vehicle, except when a shuttle is docked to it.) Three *X-38 CRVs* were built and tested by dropping them from underneath a "mothership" at an altitude of up to thirty-nine thousand feet. Due to cost overruns, however, NASA canceled the *X-38 CRV* project in 2002.

▲ A NASA illustration shows a hypothetical crew recovery vehicle at the *International Space Station*.

One of the ongoing technical advances in space suit construction is the development of a "mechanical counter pressure suit." Unlike a conventional pressurized suit, it would be a snug-fitting garment that would allow greater astronaut movement and dexterity. It would also be safer since a small tear or puncture would not cause a catastrophic depressurization.

The importance of preventing space walk accidents is more crucial today than ever before. That is because of the tremendous number of hours of work in space necessary to complete the *International Space Station*. From 1999 to its projected completion sometime after 2007, the station will require more space walk time—as many as fifteen hundred hours—than in the previous history of space exploration.

Danger from Deep Space

Reducing the risk of harm from space debris is another growing concern. Space debris includes the increasing numbers of dead satellites and other human-made materials left in orbit from half a century of space exploration. NASA tries to keep track of the largest pieces but it has estimated that more than a million objects now encircle the Earth. The potential for an accident to result from hitting one of these pieces of space debris has many space observers worried. Space shuttle orbiters have already been struck many times by meteoroids (meteor particles) and tiny pieces of human-made orbital debris. During a 1983 flight of the *Challenger*, for example, astronaut Rick Hauck reported:

> I noticed a small pit in one of the windows of the crew cabin. Spectrographic analysis of the residue left in this tiny pit revealed the presence of titanium and aluminum, suggesting that the orbiter had been hit by a chip of paint that had flaked off of some unknown spacecraft or rocket body. This was one of the first indications that orbital debris might pose a hazard to the space shuttle.[54]

Subsequent impacts have caused similarly minor damage, but the risk of catastrophe is considerable—even a tiny object can cripple a spacecraft if it hit certain vital parts. Exactly how tiny depends on a number of factors but space authorities say that as a rough guide, particles smaller than about 1/25th of an inch in size (about the thickness of the graphite in a pencil) do not pose much of a threat to a spacecraft. Debris

▼ A collision with even a small meteor could be instantly disastrous for a space shuttle orbiter or other spacecraft as this illustration shows.

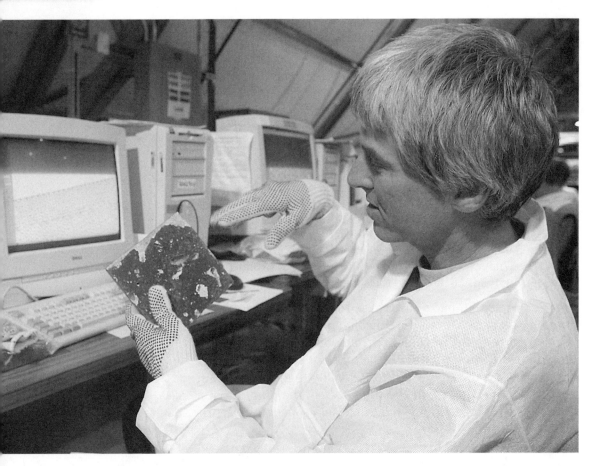

▲ The space shuttle's thermal tiles, like this one recovered from the *Columbia,* provide an uncertain defense against reentry heat.

fragments larger than that, up to about four inches in size, can penetrate a spacecraft, damage it, and possibly destroy it. Fragments larger than that, such as a six-inch-long fragment weighing about two pounds—something the size of a desktop stapler, say—would blow a three-thousand-pound satellite into a million pieces from a collision.

Space objects have such powerful effects because of how fast they are moving. The paint chip that hit the *Challenger* in 1983 may have been traveling 13,500 miles per hour. Objects in Earth orbits below about 1,200 miles may be traveling at relative velocities in excess of 20,000 miles per hour. At that speed a mere marble-sized aluminum ball hits with the force of a four-hundred-pound motorcycle traveling at 60 miles per hour.

Some space experts say that NASA should pay more attention to the survivability of the shuttle orbiter and crew in the face of the meteor and space debris hazard. Options include changing flight patterns and adding shielding to certain sections of the shuttle. These options, it should be noted, come with their own set of risks. More shielding means more weight, for example, which can make landings riskier.

Dealing with Reentry Heat

One of the most challenging inherent dangers to space travel is dealing with the physical forces upon reentering the atmosphere. While metals such as titanium and molybdenum, as well as various human-made materials, can resist the searing heat of reentry, the real technical challenge for a large space vehicle like the shuttle orbiter is that the material must be very lightweight.

Early American space capsules used a composite metal, plastic, and ceramic heat shield that dissipated heat by partially melting during reentry. Since the space shuttle's inception scientists have argued about the heat-deflection strategy that relies mainly on twenty-four thousand, one- to five-inch-deep, six-inch-square tiles cemented to the orbiters' underbellies. These ceramic tiles with a hardened-glass surface are amazingly effective at dissipating heat—it is possible to hold the edges of one in bare hands while its interior glows red hot. But they can be brittle and difficult to keep attached to the orbiter's aluminum body. The difficulty in keeping tiles attached was apparent even before an orbiter reached space. When the *Columbia* was transported, piggyback atop a specially equipped Boeing 747, from its production facility in California to Florida, for its first launch in 1981, 40 percent of the tiles flew off the spacecraft during the poky subsonic flight.

The early shuttle flights had alarmingly high failure rates for the tiles. During the first decade of the program, orbiters returned to Earth with an average of almost two hundred damaged tiles. The damage rate has since been cut in half but remains a concern because, as NASA tile researcher and risk-management specialist Elisabeth Pate-Cornell put it, "Losing a single tile can do you in."[55] Space engineers have also

DODGING BULLETS IN SPACE

While the element of chance cannot be controlled, various operational procedures can influence a spacecraft's risk of collision with meteors and space debris. On at least eight occasions, NASA has maneuvered shuttle orbiters in space to avoid a collision with objects. It is also possible to orient the space shuttle relative to its orbital path in a way that makes it a smaller target, and thus less likely to get hit by space debris. The trade-off in safety, however, may affect certain scientific experiments or other aspects of the craft's overall mission.

developed new tiles with somewhat tougher surfaces. These can be installed, however, only on the somewhat cooler areas of the orbiters' undersides.

A number of innovative new technologies are being considered as alternative approaches to dealing with the friction and heat of reentry. Among the new technologies being investigated are a system of metal panels sandwiched between insulating materials, and greater use of the carbon composites already found on leading wing edges. Researchers are also attempting to develop new "fibrous refractor composite insulation" tiles, with added silica for lightness. Another option

THE SPACE SHUTTLE'S ACHILLES' HEEL

Space engineers say that if the shuttle orbiters' heat deflection system has an especially vulnerable spot it is on the underside where seams seal off the wheel-well doors. This is the only part of the vehicle's underside that opens, allowing the landing gear to descend. "There are very important tiles under there. If you lose the tiles on those stretches . . . it can cause the shuttle to be lost," Carnegie Mellon University engineer Paul Fischbeck told NASA in an analysis he conducted in the early 1990s. Even if the result was not an immediate *Columbia*-style disaster, the damage to tires or landing mechanisms could lead to loss of control upon touchdown and a crash landing.

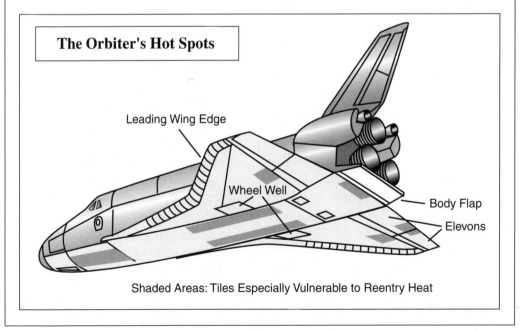

The Orbiter's Hot Spots

Leading Wing Edge

Wheel Well

Body Flap

Elevons

Shaded Areas: Tiles Especially Vulnerable to Reentry Heat

being considered is placing thermal sensors in the tiles, which would give astronauts and mission control advance notice of a possible failure. "It would be much better to know immediately when [tile failure] happens," MIT engineering professor Subra Saresh told the *Boston Globe*, "and not have to wait until reentry."[56]

Should America Scuttle the Shuttle?

Despite many recent advances in space safety practices and technologies, space shuttle accidents have now claimed more lives than all of the other U.S. and Russian human spaceflight programs in their entire history. In the wake of the catastrophic loss of the second of five shuttle vehicles, critics had a stronger case that the program eats too much of the space budget, offers little in the way of scientific knowledge, and is unacceptably dangerous.

The *Challenger* and *Columbia* disasters confirmed some of the criticisms of the shuttle program that had dogged it even before its first successful launch back in 1981. These criticisms were perhaps most forcefully compiled in Gregg Easterbrook's April 1980 article for *Washington Monthly*, entitled "Beam Me Out of This Death Trap, Scotty." Even the article's subtitle is spooky in hindsight: "5 . . . 4 . . . 3 . . . 2 . . . 1 . . . Goodbye, *Columbia*." Easterbrook marshaled an impressive array of facts and insights in contending that the shuttle would be not only a dangerous technology but also an exceedingly expensive one. Many of his predictions—especially that fifty routine launches annually, and a catastrophe rate of one in 2,500, would turn out to be pipe dreams—have proven correct. The shuttle has never flown more than eight missions in a year and its catastrophe rate now stands at one in fifty-seven.

The shuttle remains extremely popular with many people, not only within NASA but among space enthusiasts, scientists, and others. Retired NASA engineer and *Rocket Boys* author Homer Hickam lamented the loss of "a national asset" after the *Columbia* accident. But he also noted that NASA should reconsider funding the development of an "orbital space plane." This would be a much simpler and lighter machine compared to the shuttle, with only one purpose: transporting crew to and from orbit. "This doesn't mean that the shuttles should immediately go away," Hickam said, "but

▲ This NASA illustration of an orbiter docked beneath the *International Space Station* underscores the importance the space agency puts on the shuttle program, despite its risks.

it does make sense to go forward with machines that allow us to do all that the shuttle does without being completely grounded when there's a mishap."[57]

Despite the *Columbia* accident, in the short term it seems unlikely that the U.S. government will decide to end the space shuttle program. NASA's most recent plans and budget requests have called for increased spending on the shuttle, allowing the orbiters to remain active for as long as the next two decades. This would provide space engineers more time to develop the next generation of spacecraft, whether to continue space station missions or to undertake an ambitious manned flight to Mars.

Toward Acceptable Risk

"Mankind never gains anything without cost," the famous Russian cosmonaut Yuri Gagarin remarked in the aftermath of Vladimir Komarov's fatal plunge to Earth onboard *Soyuz 1*. "There has never been a bloodless victory over nature."[58] Gagarin himself was killed within a year, in March 1968, from a plane crash during a training mission. His feelings about the need to embrace the risks of space exploration nevertheless live on. After the *Columbia* accident, even members of the dead astronauts' families were among those who said that the space program should continue, regardless of the cost in human lives. According to NASA administrator Sean O'Keefe:

> There is a larger issue that we may need to debate: is the risk of space exploration something we really want to examine in a broader public context where we weigh [the benefits of space exploration] against what we think this vehicle portends in terms of its risk—and whether that is acceptable or not.[59]

In other words, given that space exploration is an inherently hazardous undertaking and that accidents can never be totally eliminated, is the public willing to continue to sacrifice lives to the effort? Certainly the space program has contributed some practical benefits, helping to develop new technologies ranging from cordless power tools to product bar coding. Some of the research experiments done in space have contributed to scientific advances.

Yet the very names of the shuttle orbiters—*Columbia, Challenger, Discovery, Atlantis, Endeavour,* taken from historic sea vessels that explored new routes and pioneered new research—suggest that the potential benefits from pursuing a space program go much deeper than products or even new knowledge. Human space flight at its core represents an exhilarating quest for discovery for its own sake, for a testing of the human spirit. Men and women seek to explore space for the same reason that the early twentieth century British climber George Mallory was willing to risk (and lose) his life to climb Mount Everest: "Because it's there." Space accidents that claim lives are tragic, but at this point humanity seems to accept that it would be even more tragic to abandon the pursuit of an endless frontier.

Notes

Introduction: Nightmares of Space

1. Gregg Easterbrook, "Beam Me Out of This Death Trap, Scotty," *Washington Monthly*, April 1980. www.washingtonmonthly.com.
2. Michael E. Long, "Surviving in Space," *National Geographic*, January 2001, p. 7.
3. Quoted in Long, *National Geographic*, p. 20.

Chapter 1: Into the Dead Zone

4. Mark Williams, "Space Was the Place, Says Old NASA Hand," *Red Herring*, July 2000. www.redherring.com.
5. T.A. Heppenheimer, *Countdown: A History of Space Flight.* New York: John Wiley, 1999, p. 218.
6. Quoted in "The Whirligig," History Office, *NASA.* www.hq.nasa.gov.
7. Quoted in David J. Shayler, *Disasters and Accidents in Manned Spaceflight.* London: Springer-Praxis, 2000, p. 247.
8. Gene Kranz, *Failure Is Not an Option.* New York: Simon and Schuster, 2000, p. 11.
9. Quoted in *Report of Apollo 204 Review Board*, "Part V: Investigation and Analyses," NASA Historical Reference Collection, NASA. www.hq.nasa.gov.
10. Quoted in Courtney G. Brooks, James M. Grimwood, and Loyd S. Swenson Jr., *Chariots for Apollo: A History of Manned Lunar Spacecraft.* Washington, DC: NASA SP-4205, 1979. www.hq.nasa.gov.
11. Quoted in *Report of Apollo 204 Review Board*, "Part V." www.hq.nasa.gov.
12. Brooks et al., *Chariots for Apollo.* www.hq.nasa.gov.
13. Kranz, *Failure Is Not an Option*, p. 11.
14. *Report of Apollo 204 Review Board*, "Summary." www.hq.nasa.gov.

15. James Oberg, *Uncovering Soviet Disasters.* New York: Random House, 1988, p. 172.

16. Shayler, *Disasters and Accidents in Manned Spaceflight,* p. 386.

17. Brooks et al., *Chariots for Apollo.* www.hq.nasa.gov.

18. David S.F. Portree, "Part 1 Soyuz," *Mir Hardware Heritage.* Washington, DC: NASA RP-1357, 1995, p. 23.

Chapter 2: A Pair of Shuttle Disasters

19. *Ronald Reagan Presidential Library,* "Announcement of United States Government Support for Private Sector Commercial Operations of Expendable Launch Vehicles," May 16, 1983. www.reagan.utexas.edu.

20. *NASA,* "Transcript of the Challenger Crew Comments from the Operational Recorder." www.hq.nasa.gov.

21. Quoted in Mark Carreau, "A Decade Since Disaster: 'I Knew Something Was Terribly Wrong,'" *Houston Chronicle,* January 29, 1996. www.chron.com.

22. Quoted in "They Slipped the Surly Bonds of Earth to Touch the Face of God," *Time,* February 10, 1986. www.time.com.

23. Quoted in Ted Bridis, "NASA Flight Director E-Mailed to Assure Columbia Astronauts," *Boston Globe,* July 1, 2003, p. A12.

24. *CNN.com,* "Transcript: Final, Frantic Minutes in Mission Control," February 17, 2003. www.cnn.com.

25. Quoted in Jeffrey Kluger, "Those Last Few Seconds," *Time,* March 24, 2003, p. 57.

26. *CNN.com,* "Transcript," www.cnn.com.

27. Mark Cantrell and Donald Vaughan, *Sixteen Minutes from Home: The Columbia Space Shuttle Tragedy.* Boca Raton, FL: American Media, 2003, pp. 5–6.

Chapter 3: Rescue Efforts

28. Quoted in Thomas H. Maugh II, "NASA Can't Mount Rescue on Re-entry," *Orlando Sentinel,* February 3, 2003. www.orlandosentinel.com.

29. Quoted in Warren E. Leary, "NASA Chief Disputes Idea That Space Shuttle Was Hopeless," *The New York Times,* February 28, 2003. www.nytimes.com.

30. Maugh, "NASA Can't Mount Rescue on Re-entry," *Orlando Sentinel.*

31. Quoted in Marcia Dunn, "Shuttle Rescue Might or Might Not Have Been Successful," *Space.com*, May 23, 2003. www.space.com.

32. Quoted in "Disaster in Space," *PBS Online NewsHour*, February 3, 2003. www.pbs.org.

33. Quoted in "Saga of the Liberty Bell," *Time*, July 28, 1961, p. 35.

34. Paul Perry, "Diving for Spacecraft: One Man's Quest to Raise NASA's Liberty Bell 7 Brings a Flood of Memories to the Surface," *Astronomy*, October 2001, p. 34.

35. Shayler, *Disasters and Accidents in Manned Spaceflight*, p. 367.

36. Quoted in *NASA*, "Detailed Chronology of Events Surrounding the *Apollo 13* Accident." www.hq.nasa.gov.

37. Quoted in Kranz, *Failure Is Not an Option*, p. 313.

38. Bryan Burrough, *Dragonfly: NASA and the Crisis Aboard Mir.* New York: HarperCollins, 1998, p. 373.

Chapter 4: Challenging Investigations

39. *Report of Apollo 204 Review Board*, "Part V." www.hq.nasa.gov.

40. Quoted in Raja Mishra, "Lead Investigator Issues Warning to NASA Officials," *Boston Globe*, February 12, 2003, p. A3.

41. *SpaceRef.com*, "STS-107 JSC MER Daily Reports." www.spaceref.com.

42. Quoted in R. Jeffrey Smith, "Mistakes of NASA Toted Up," *Washington Post*, July 13, 2003. www.washingtonpost.com.

43. *Columbia Accident Investigation Board*, "Foam Impact Test Breaks Reinforced Carbon-Carbon Panel," June 6, 2003. www.caib.us.

44. Quoted in Marcia Dunn, "Shuttle Foam Test Offers 'Smoking Gun' Proof Of Disaster," *Space.com*, July 7, 2003. www.space.com.

45. Smith, "Mistakes of NASA Toted Up," *Washington Post.*

46. James Oberg, "The Hole in NASA's Safety Culture," *MSNBC News*, July 8, 2003. www.msnbc.com.

47. Quoted in Shankar Vedantam, "Cultural Divide Plagues NASA," *Washington Post*, February 10, 2003. www.washingtonpost.com.

48. Edward Clinton Ezell and Linda Neuman Ezell, *The Partnership: A History of the Apollo-Soyuz Test Project*, "Mid-Term Review." Washington, DC: NASA SP-4209, 1978. www.hq.nasa.gov.

Chapter 5: Preventing Future Accidents

49. *RussianSpaceWeb.com*, "Rockets: R-16 Family: Nedelin Disaster." www.russianspaceweb.com.

50. James Oberg, "Software Bug Sent Soyuz Off Course," *MSNBC News*, May 5, 2003. www.msnbc.com.

51. Quoted in Shayler, *Disasters and Accidents in Manned Spaceflight*, p. 167.

52. Lydia Dotto, "'Deep Diving' in Space: Spacewalking Astronauts Risk Getting 'Bent'," *Spacenet*. www.spacenet.on.ca.

53. Quoted in Todd Halvorson, "Astronauts Cap 100th Spacewalk with Successful Disaster Drill," *Space.com*, February 14, 2001. www.space.com.

54. Quoted in *National Academy Press*, "Protecting the Space Shuttle from Meteoroids and Orbital Debris," Press Committee on Space Shuttle Meteoroid/Debris Risk Management. Washington, DC: National Research Council, 1997. www.nap.edu.

55. Quoted in "Spaceship Columbia," LUNAR'clips 2003, *Livermore Unit of the National Association of Rocketry*, January/February 2003. www.lunar.org.

56. Quoted in Gareth Cook, "Keeping the Heat Outside the Shuttle," *Boston Globe*, February 4, 2003, p. C4.

57. Homer Hickam, "Space Shuttle Columbia: Goodbye to a Good Old Girl," *SpaceRef.com*, February 7, 2003. www.spaceref.com.

58. Quoted in Burrough, *Dragonfly*, p. 80.

59. Quoted in Keith Cowling, "Safety Panel to NASA: Build a 'Full Envelope' Shuttle Escape System," *SpaceRef.com*, March 26, 2003. www.spaceref.com.

Glossary

astronaut: A crew member or passenger aboard a spacecraft.

attitude: The position or orientation of a spacecraft in relation to a specific direction or reference point, such as the horizon or a particular star.

Baikonur Cosmodrome: The Russian Space Agency's main launch site for manned missions, located in the Republic of Kazakhstan.

booster: The first stage of a missile or rocket.

Cape Canaveral: NASA's main launch site, on Florida's east coast; officially renamed Cape Kennedy from 1963 to 1973, though the center is still called John F. Kennedy Space Center.

command module: The compartment of a spacecraft that contains the crew and main controls; it acts as the spacecraft's reentry vehicle.

cosmonaut: The Russian term for an astronaut.

dock: The linking up of two spacecraft while in space.

escape velocity: The speed necessary to escape the gravitational field of a planet or other body in space; the escape velocity from the Earth's surface is approximately seven miles per second.

external tank: In the space shuttle program, the source of the liquid fuel for the orbiter's three main rocket engines.

hatch: A door or doorway on a spacecraft, sealed but armed with small detonators for emergency exit.

heat shield: A panel or other device that protects a capsule from the heat generated by friction with the atmosphere upon reentry.

launchpad: A reinforced base from which a rocket can be fired.

liftoff: The blast-off of a rocket from its launchpad.

lunar: Of or pertaining to the Moon.

lunar module: The part of the Apollo mission spacecraft that landed on the Moon and returned to the orbiting command module.

multistage rocket: A rocket with two or more stages; each stage falls away from the remaining craft after it has finished its firing.

NASA: National Aeronautics and Space Administration, the American government's official space agency since 1958.

orbiter: In the space shuttle program, the jet-like winged spacecraft, such as the *Challenger* and *Columbia*, that carries the payload and crew into space and eventually glides back to Earth.

pressure suit: A suit and helmet that can be inflated to provide body pressure and air to breathe when a spacecraft leaves the Earth's atmosphere.

reentry: The descent into Earth's atmosphere from space, causing aerodynamic friction and thus generating tremendous heat.

rocket: A missile or vehicle propelled forward or upward due to the ejected exhaust products of fuel and oxygen combustion.

solid rocket booster: In the space shuttle program, the two narrow, solid-fuel rockets that provide about 70 percent of launch power.

space: The universe beyond the Earth's atmosphere, which ends at approximately seventy to one hundred miles above the Earth's surface.

spacecraft: Vehicles rocket-launched into space, including satellites and space probes as well as manned missions.

space debris: Human-made objects or discarded junk left in space.

space shuttle: The American space project consisting of rocket boosters, disposable external tanks for liftoff, and the reusable orbiters *Endeavour, Discovery*, and *Atlantis* (*Challenger* and *Columbia* have been destroyed).

space station: An orbiting spacecraft designed to support human activity for an extended time.

thermal tile: The silica fiber insulated squares used to protect much of the exterior of space shuttle orbiters against the intense heat generated upon reentry.

For Further Reading

Books

Mark Cantrell and Donald Vaughan, *Sixteen Minutes from Home: The Columbia Space Shuttle Tragedy*. Boca Raton, FL: American Media, 2003. This timely paperback focuses on the major characters and events.

T.A. Heppenheimer, *Countdown: A History of Space Flight*. New York: John Wiley, 1999. Offers a lively narrative account of the space age.

Gene Kranz, *Failure Is Not an Option*. New York: Simon and Schuster, 2000. The heyday of the American space program from the perspective of a prominent flight director.

Periodicals

Nancy Gibbs, "Seven Astronauts, One Fate," *Time*, February 10, 2003.

Michael E. Long, "Surviving in Space," *National Geographic*, January 2001.

Internet Sources

Gregg Easterbrook, "Beam Me Out of This Death Trap, Scotty," *Washington Monthly*, April 1980. www.washingtonmonthly.com.

NASA, "Detailed Chronology of Events Surrounding the *Apollo 13* Accident." www.hq.nasa.gov.

Time, "They Slipped the Surly Bonds of Earth to Touch the Face of God," February 10, 1986. www.time.com.

Shankar Vedantam, "Cultural Divide Plagues NASA," *Washington Post*, February 10, 2003. www.washingtonpost.com.

Websites

Columbia Accident Investigation Board (www.caib.us). The official investigation site.

National Aeronautics and Space Administration (www.nasa.gov). Offers a huge volume of background information on the space program, including its accidents and incidents.

Works Consulted

Books

Bryan Burrough, *Dragonfly: NASA and the Crisis Aboard Mir.* New York: HarperCollins, 1998. A harrowing account of one space crisis after another.

James R. Chiles, *Inviting Disaster: Lessons from the Leading Edge of Technology.* New York: HarperBusiness, 2002. A fascinating look at how catastrophes happen, including the *Challenger* disaster.

James Oberg, *Uncovering Soviet Disasters.* New York: Random House, 1988. Provides useful background information on a number of Soviet space accidents.

Charles Perrow, *Normal Accidents: Living with High-Risk Technologies.* Princeton, NJ: Princeton University Press, 1999. Why complex technologies, including space missions, sometimes fail.

David J. Shayler, *Disasters and Accidents in Manned Spaceflight.* London: Springer-Praxis, 2000. A wide-ranging and authoritative technical work.

Periodicals

Aerospace Safety Advisory Panel, *Annual Report for 2002.* Washington, DC: NASA, 2003.

Ted Bridis, "NASA Flight Director E-Mailed to Assure Columbia Astronauts," *Boston Globe*, July 1, 2003.

Gareth Cook, "Keeping the Heat Outside the Shuttle," *Boston Globe*, February 4, 2003.

Mark Jurkowitz, "In Contrast with '86, Agency Viewed as Responsive to Inquiries," *Boston Globe*, February 6, 2003.

Jeffrey Kluger, "Those Last Few Seconds," *Time*, March 24, 2003.

Raja Mishra, "Lead Investigator Issues Warning to NASA Officials," *Boston Globe*, February 12, 2003.

Paul Perry, "Diving for Spacecraft: One Man's Quest to Raise NASA's Liberty Bell 7 Brings a Flood of Memories to the Surface," *Astronomy*, October 2001.

David S.F. Portree, "Part 1 Soyuz," *Mir Hardware Heritage.* Washington, DC: NASA RP-1357, 1995.

"Saga of the Liberty Bell," *Time*, July 28, 1961.

Dan Vergano and Tim Friend, "Upper Atmosphere May Hold Clues in Columbia Mystery," *USA Today*, February 7, 2003.

Internet Sources

BBC Online Network, "A Silent Death," July 10, 1999. http://news.bbc.co.uk.

CNN.com, "Transcript: Final, Frantic Minutes in Mission Control," February 17, 2003. www.cnn.com.

Courtney G. Brooks, James M. Grimwood, and Loyd S. Swenson Jr., *Chariots for Apollo: A History of Manned Lunar Spacecraft.* Washington, DC: NASA SP-4205, 1979. www.hq.nasa.gov.

Mark Carreau, "A Decade Since Disaster: 'I Knew Something Was Terribly Wrong,'" *Houston Chronicle*, January 29, 1996. www.chron.com.

Columbia Accident Investigation Board, "Foam Impact Test Breaks Reinforced Carbon-Carbon Panel," June 6, 2003. www.caib.us.

Keith Cowling, "Safety Panel to NASA: Build a 'Full Envelope' Shuttle Escape System," *SpaceRef.com*, March 26, 2003. www.spaceref.com.

Lydia Dotto, "'Deep Diving' in Space: Spacewalking Astronauts Risk Getting 'Bent'," *Spacenet*. www.spacenet. on.ca.

Marcia Dunn, "Shuttle Rescue Might or Might Not Have Been Successful," *Space.com*, May 23, 2003. www.space. com.

————"Shuttle Foam Test Offers 'Smoking Gun' Proof Of Disaster," *Space.com*, July 7, 2003. www.space.com.

Edward Clinton Ezell and Linda Neuman Ezell, *The Partnership: A History of the Apollo-Soyuz Test Project.* Washington, DC: NASA SP-4209, 1978. www.hq.nasa.gov.

Todd Halvorson, "Astronauts Cap 100th Spacewalk with Successful Disaster Drill," *Space.com*, February 14, 2001. www.space.com.

————"'Go Fever' and Challenger Lessons: Agency Chooses Safety Over Schedule," *Space.com*, January 19, 2001. www.space.com.

Homer Hickam, "Space Shuttle Columbia: Goodbye to a Good Old Girl," *SpaceRef.com*, February 7, 2003. www.spaceref.com.

Warren E. Leary, "NASA Chief Disputes Idea That Space Shuttle Was Hopeless," *The New York Times*, February 28, 2003. www.nytimes.com.

Livermore Unit of the National Association of Rocketry, LUNAR'clips 2003, January/February 2003, "Spaceship Columbia." www.lunar.org.

Thomas H. Maugh II, "NASA Can't Mount Rescue on Re-entry," *Orlando Sentinel*, February 3, 2003. www.orlandosentinel.com.

NASA, "Joseph P. Kerwin to Richard H. Truly, July 28, 1986." www.hq.nasa.gov.

————"Transcript of the Challenger Crew Comments from the Operational Recorder." www.hq.nasa.gov.

————History Office, "The Whirligig." www.hq.nasa.gov.

National Academy Press, "Protecting the Space Shuttle from Meteoroids and Orbital Debris," Press Committee on Space Shuttle Meteoroid/Debris Risk Management. Washington, DC: National Research Council, 1997. www.nap.edu.

James Oberg, "Consultant Report: Soyuz Landing Safety," *JamesOberg.com*. March 19, 1997. www.jamesoberg.com.

————"The Hole in NASA's Safety Culture," *MSNBC News*, July 8, 2003. www.msnbc.com.

————"Software Bug Sent Soyuz Off Course," *MSNBC News*, May 5, 2003. www.msnbc.com.

PBS Online NewsHour, "Disaster in Space," February 3, 2003. www.pbs.org.

Paul Recer, "NASA Defends Use of Heat Tiles on Shuttles," *Space.com*, February 5, 2003. www.space.com.

Report of Apollo 204 Review Board, "Part V: Investigation and Analyses," NASA Historical Reference Collection, NASA. www.hq.nasa.gov.

Ronald Reagan Presidential Library, "Announcement of United States Government Support for Private Sector Commercial Operations of Expendable Launch Vehicles," May 16, 1983. www.reagan.utexas.edu.

RussianSpaceWeb.com, "Rockets: R-16 Family: Nedelin Disaster." www.russianspaceweb.com.

R. Jeffrey Smith, "Mistakes of NASA Toted Up," *Washington Post*, July 13, 2003. www.washingtonpost.com.

Smithsonian National Air and Space Museum, "Bachem Ba 349B-1 Natter (BP-20)." www.nasm.si.edu.

SpaceRef.com, "STS-107 JSC MER Daily Reports," www.spaceref.com.

Mark Williams, "Space Was the Place Says Old NASA Hand," *Red Herring*, July 2000. www.redherring.com.

Websites

Aviation Week & Space Technology (www.aviationnow.com). Excellent space reporting, with even more available to subscribers.

Space.com (www.space.com). Handsomely produced and informative.

Index

Picture Credits

About the Author

Mark Mayell is a freelance writer and editor who has authored nonfiction books on health and travel, as well as Man-Made Disasters: *Nuclear Accidents*. He lives with his wife and two children in Wellesley, Massachusetts.